HENRY WARD BEECHER'S
ART OF PREACHING

THE UNIVERSITY OF CHICAGO PRESS
CHICAGO, ILLINOIS

—

THE BAKER & TAYLOR COMPANY
NEW YORK

THE CAMBRIDGE UNIVERSITY PRESS
LONDON

THE MARUZEN-KABUSHIKI-KAISHA
TOKYO, OSAKA, KYOTO, FUKUOKA, SENDAI

THE COMMERCIAL PRESS, LIMITED
SHANGHAI

HENRY WARD BEECHER'S ART OF PREACHING

By

LIONEL GEORGE CROCKER

Denison University

THE UNIVERSITY OF CHICAGO PRESS
CHICAGO · ILLINOIS

COMPOSED AND PRINTED BY THE UNIVERSITY OF CHICAGO PRESS
CHICAGO, ILLINOIS, U.S.A.

DEDICATED TO
GERALDINE HAMILTON CROCKER, M.D

22450

PREFACE

In preparing this manuscript for publication there was a temptation to make it popular by employing more biographical and illustrative material, and by giving a comparison of Henry Ward Beecher with his contemporaries in the pulpit. However, the danger of obscuring Henry Ward Beecher's art of preaching lurked in such a revision. I also felt that those students who would be attracted to this little volume are already familiar with his background and work. As the study stands, the reader will find that I have attempted to confine my research to the following limits: to formulate the rhetorical theory of Henry Ward Beecher as expressed by him in the *Yale Lectures* and elsewhere; to illustrate briefly this theory with examples from his works; and to evaluate it in relation to past and present rhetorical theory.

It is a pleasure to extend my thanks to Professor J. M. O'Neill, Professor R. W. Cowden, Dr. L. M. Eich, Dr. J. H. Muyskens, and Dr. C. D. Thorpe, all of the University of Michigan, who put their learning at my disposal; to Dr. J. Stanley Durkee, who gave me the keys to the Plymouth Church library and archives; and to President Avery A. Shaw of Denison University, who helped me in ways he knows not of.

Granville, Ohio
January, 1934

LIONEL GEORGE CROCKER

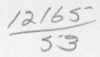

TABLE OF CONTENTS

INTRODUCTION

A. Origin of the problem
B. Importance
C. Materials
D. Method

A

This study of the rhetorical theory of Henry Ward Beecher is the outgrowth of an attempt begun several years ago to state and evaluate the rhetorical theory contained in the entire series of *The Yale Lectures on Preaching*.[1] I discovered that in this project there was too much material for my purpose. There are volumes of lectures for every year, with one or two exceptions, from 1872 to the present time. Being faced with so much material, and being unwilling to give up altogether the idea of studying the *Yale Lectures on Preaching*, I decided to focus my attention upon one of the series of lectures. As I studied the many volumes, I became more and more impressed with the possibilities of the initial series by Henry Ward Beecher, and I decided to limit my study to his lectures. The reasons for this choice I shall try to make clear.

[1] This series of lectures was endowed by Mr. Henry Sage, a parishioner of Henry Ward Beecher and an admirer of his genius. This series is known as "The Lyman Beecher Lectureship on Preaching," in honor of Henry Ward Beecher's distinguished father. It is safe to say that if it had not been for Henry Ward Beecher, the *Yale Lectures on Preaching*, which have so greatly enriched the literature of preaching, would never have been given. Mr. Sage was desirous of giving young men who were studying for the ministry the benefit of Henry Ward Beecher's successful experience in the pulpit. To this end, it was arranged for Henry Ward Beecher to give the first lectures at Yale College before the Theological Department in 1872. He gave them in three successive years. They appeared in book form in 1872, 1873, and in 1874. In 1896 they appeared in one volume.

B

At the outset, such a study seemed promising. Here was an artist conversing about his art, for Beecher believed that preaching was a useful art. Preaching proceeded according to rules which had to be studied. One had to serve his apprentice-ship. To discover what principles Beecher thought were in-volved in effective preaching became a matter of interest. It is not often that one has the opportunity of looking behind the scenes to discover how the effects are obtained by such a pulpit orator as Henry Ward Beecher.

How far were these principles a part of the rhetorical tradi-tion became a fascinating query. From a number of sugges-tions it appeared that Beecher thought of rhetoric as the facul-ty of finding the instruments of persuasion, a phrase used several times by him in the course of his *Yale Lectures*.[2] Some of Beecher's statements seemed reminiscent of Whately. Others seemed to be governed by Herbert Spencer's "principle of economy." There seemed possible parallels to De Quincey. These observations challenged further inquiry.

The rhetorical matters considered by Beecher appeared inter-esting and important. Since Beecher[3] regarded the sermon as the most momentous of the duties of a Christian minister, would one not expect to find some observations on its construction that would merit investigation? Like Plato, Beecher believed that the preacher must understand all kinds and conditions of men. One entire lecture is devoted to the significance of a study of human nature by the preacher; and, moreover, the necessity of viewing all rhetorical problems from the viewpoint of the audience seemed to permeate his rhetorical theory.

---

[2] This phrase, "instruments of persuasion," occurs several times in the *Yale Lectures* (1st ser.), pp. 3, 7, 29, 178, and 185.

[3] *Yale Lectures* (1st ser.), p. 29.

Beecher appeared to be urging a study of the psychology of appeals to an audience. No student of rhetoric can read, even casually, through his lecture on the illustration and remain indifferent to his penetrative insight into this instrument of persuasion. Beecher's statement that he cultivated the use of the illustration gave a hint as to his study of rhetoric. The importance he attached to the imaginative process stimulated my interest. These and other matters pertaining to the invention of the sermon attracted me to a study of Beecher.

The suggestions dropped by Beecher for the planning of sermons arrested my attention. Again, it appeared that the audience seemed to play an essential part in determining the form of the discourse. Suggestions as to the form of a sermon designed to reach the common people seemed pertinent enough to require further investigation.

That style, Beecher believed, is best for the public speaker that contemplates a body of listeners. This was penetrating and important. I had often had my attention drawn to quotations from Beecher that owed their effectiveness as much to their phrasing as to their truth. Beecher's theory of style invited closer attention.

Beecher's usefulness as a subject of rhetorical study was further increased by the large number of references to him as a source of rhetorical precept and illustration. And, although the rhetorical influence[4] of Beecher is outside the scope of the present study, such quotation indicated indirectly the rhetorical worth of his *Yale Lectures*. For years I have been impressed with the quotations from Beecher's lecture on illustrations appearing in well-known textbooks on public speaking. For instance, E. D. Shurter, *The Rhetoric of Oratory* (1907), and J. A. Broadus, *The Preparation and Delivery of the Sermon* (revised

[4] Cf. Lionel Crocker, "The Rhetorical Influence of Henry Ward Beecher," *Quarterly Journal of Speech*, XVIII (February, 1932), 82–87.

ed., 1898), and W. N. Brigance, *The Spoken Word* (1927), to mention no others, substantiate their own remarks on the illustration with liberal quotations from Beecher's lecture. George Pierce Baker's *Principles of Argumentation* (1895) employed the "Liverpool Address" as a splendid example of persuasion before a hostile audience. No prominent book on argumentation since that time has omitted reference to the "Liverpool Address."

In making such a study I am on new ground. The life of Henry Ward Beecher has proved a theme for many writers. Interesting aspects of this orator's life as it related itself to the slavery problem and the Civil War have been adequately narrated. In such biographical studies there has been agreement that the *Yale Lectures on Preaching* are of first importance in Beecher's prodigious output, but such comment has been limited to praise, with no systematic attempt to present and analyze the rhetorical theory contained in them. For instance, J. H. Barrows[5] states, "Foremost among Beecher's works, I mention 'The Yale Lectures on Preaching' which remain unsurpassed in suggestiveness and stimulating power." In a similar laudatory vein is the passage in Lyman Abbott's[6] chapter on "The Yale Lectures." Lyman Abbott stated that these lectures were the best work Beecher ever did. T. W. Knox[7] devotes a chapter to these lectures, but is content with a pleasing résumé rather than an evaluation.

C

While the *Yale Lectures* are the most important of Beecher's works pertaining to rhetorical matters, they are not the only

[5] J. H. Barrows, *The Shakespeare of the Pulpit* (New York, 1893), p. x.

[6] Lyman Abbott, *Henry Ward Beecher* (New York, 1903), p. 273.

[7] T. W. Knox, *Life and Works of Henry Ward Beecher* (Cincinnati, Ohio, 1887), chap. xvii.

ones dealing with the thought and language aspects of the sermon. Besides his *Yale Lectures on Preaching*, three series (1872-73-74), there is *Successful Preaching* (1870), *Lecture on Oratory* (1876), *Address to Students* (1886), and *True Preaching* (1886). It should be pointed out that these lectures are not studied statements of rhetorical theory but familiar talks on aspects of preaching drawn from his own rich experience. Like Cicero in *De oratore*, Beecher did not design to set forth a system of rhetoric but to communicate to men some practical hints drawn from his own successful practice. Speaking of illustrations, he said, "It is not my province to go into the theoretical nature of the different kinds of illustrations, of metaphors, similes, and what not; that you have learned in another department both in your academical and collegiate courses. But I hope to give you some practical hints as to the manner of using these things." It is from these practical hints that one must formulate Beecher's rhetorical theory.

In order to evaluate Beecher's rhetorical theory I have used those treatises on rhetoric that usually appear in any discussion of the history of rhetorical thought. Among the ancients, I have consulted Plato, Aristotle, Cicero, and Quintilian. Among the English rhetoricians, I have consulted Cox, Wilson, Campbell, Blair, Kames, Whately, Bain, Herbert Spencer, and De Quincey. Of the critics, I have employed Coleridge and Wordsworth. Of the rhetorical writings of our own day I have employed, chiefly, the essays in Lane Cooper's *Theories of Style*, the essays in W. T. Brewster's *Representative Essays on Style*, other volumes of the *Yale Lectures on Preaching*, the writings of Fred Newton Scott, and the texts of A. E. Phillips, J. A. Winans, J. M. O'Neill, and A. T. Weaver. Besides these, I have had occasion to refer to numerous other texts and articles which will be found in the body of the thesis.

D

The traditional divisions of rhetoric, invention, arrangement, and style, have been followed as the major divisions of the thesis. The method has been expository and comparative. I have first sought to state Beecher's rhetorical theory, and, then, to illustrate it from his practice; and, finally, to compare the rhetorical principles involved with the past and present statements of the same principles. The relative worth of Beecher's rhetorical theory will thus be shown, and, moreover, if Beecher added anything to our understanding of the problem of literary composition, it will be discovered. In proceeding in this manner, I have often quoted at length from Beecher's works as the best possible evidence to support and illustrate my point.

INVENTION

A. Sources of materials
  1. Life
    a) First-hand study
    b) The common people
  2. Books
    a) Literature
    b) Rhetorical theory
    c) Science
  3. Physical nature
  4. Art
B. The creative process
  1. Lifelong preparation
  2. Brooding
  3. Immediate preparation
  4. Act of speaking
C. Proofs peculiar to preaching
  1. Ethical
  2. Pathetic
  3. Logical

A

In the present division, under the head of Invention, I wish to consider the process of gathering materials employed by Beecher; to examine his method of synthesizing these materials; and to study the nature of the proof used by him in his preaching. In short, invention, as I shall treat it, concerns the mustering of the instruments of persuasion up to the point of arrangement.

Materials must come primarily from a first-hand knowledge of life, Beecher declared. As in Aristotle's *Rhetoric*, the necessity of knowing human nature runs like a thread throughout the rhetorical theory of Beecher. His own preaching as a young man in Indianapolis was unsuccessful until he realized that he did not know the needs of his congregation. Preaching is unsuccessful that does not adapt[1] itself to the wants of the congregation. He searched the scriptures and discovered that successful preaching was predicated on beginning with what the audience knew. He made a list of these "you all knows,"[2] and built his preaching upon them. He is speaking out of his own experience when he says, "A man may know the Bible from Genesis to Revelation, he may know every theological treatise from the day of St. Augustine to Dr. Taylor, and if he does not know human nature he is not fit to preach."[3] He devotes a lecture[4] of twenty-seven pages to impressing the young men at Yale Theological School with the importance of a first-hand study of human nature.

Like Walt Whitman,[5] his Brooklyn friend and admirer, Beecher was accustomed to ride in the driver's seat on the tops of omnibuses or in the pilot's cab on ferry boats in order to learn life direct. In this way, the great current of human

[1] The necessity of adaptation of the message to the congregation is repeated on pages 6, 7, 36, 51, 53, 59, 209, 221, and 235 of the *Yale Lectures* (1st ser.).

[2] Beecher regarded this discovery as the turning point in his success as a preacher. Before appearing in the *Yale Lectures*, the anecdote is given in *Eyes and Ears*, p. 110 (1862). It appears again in the *Yale Lectures* (2d ser.), p. 299; and, again, in *Address to Students* (1886).

[3] *Yale Lectures* (1st ser.), p. 85.

[4] Oliver Wendell Holmes states the thought Beecher had in mind thus: "I believe in life rather than in books. I suppose every day of earth, with its hundred thousand deaths and something more of births, with its loves and hates, its triumphs and defeats, its pangs and blisses, has more of humanity in it than all the books that were ever written, put together." *The Autocrat of the Breakfast Table* (New York, 1858), p. 134.

[5] Clara Barrus, *Whitman and Burroughs, Comrades* (New York, 1931): "We have much talk, and it does me good to be with him again. He (Whitman) talks affectionately of Beecher, just dead, and says many things in his praise. Beecher was very cordial to him" (p. 264).

life supplied him with materials for his sermons. Respect for his fellow-men was based upon intimate acquaintance.

Now, I take great delight, if ever I can get a chance, in riding on the top of an omnibus with the driver and talking with him. What do I gain by that? Why my sympathy goes out for these men, and I recognize in them an element of brotherhood,—that great element which lies underneath all culture, which is more universal and more important than all special attributes which is the great generic bond of humanity between man and man. If ever I saw one of these men in my church, I could preach to him, and hit him under the rib with an illustration, much better than if I had not been acquainted with him.[6]

Beecher browsed as much upon men as some preachers browse upon books. He lived in an era of great ideas and in talking with men he came to feel the great movements of the time. He learned what the pulse of the people was.

In studying people, Beecher sought out the habits of the common people,[7] a phrase used by him many times in the course of the *Yale Lectures*. In this emphasis, he, no doubt, believed he had scriptural authority, for Jesus Christ, we are told, was heard gladly by the common people. Like a scientist, Beecher narrowed his field of appeal. He determined at the beginning his audience level and gauged his appeals accordingly. He counseled the young preachers, "If you are going to be a minister, keep very close to the plain people; don't get above the common people."[8] Even in the structure of his church Beecher kept the taste of the common people in mind.[9] His

[6] *Yale Lectures* (1st ser.), p. 98.

[7] In the *Yale Lectures* (1st ser.), Beecher refers to the necessity of reaching the common people in the following pages: 98, 147, 163, 169, 181, 200, 208, 219, 226, 231, 232, 234. In addition to these references, the following addresses stress the importance of studying the common people: *The Ground and Form of Government, The Success of American Democracy*, and the *Address to Students*.

[8] *Yale Lectures* (1st ser.), p. 98.

[9] For an excellent description of Beecher's church see James Parton, *Famous Americans of Recent Times* (Boston, 1877), pp. 347-72.

love for the common people was a lifelong passion. In his popular lyceum address entitled "The Wastes and Burdens of Society," he declared, "The test of civilization is not at the top,
it is at the average, but more especially at the bottom of society." Such a philosophy filled his church, as would be expected, with the common people, just as he desired. His appeal to the masses was noted by Barrett Wendell[10] who stated
that Beecher's sway, though wide, was not among the influential classes. In another of his successful lyceum addresses, entitled, "The Reign of the Common People," not only is the
title significant, but also the expressed doctrine.[11] When giving
this address in England, he said:

You are educating the top, we are educating society from the bottom
to the top; we are not attempting to lift favoured classes higher, we are
attempting to put our hands under the foundations of human life, and
lift everybody up. This is slower work but when it is done you will never
doubt again which is the wisest and best policy.

This belief in democracy and its program is the fundamental
thesis upon which Beecher based his appeals to his audience.

Beecher's faith in the masses was matched by that other
wheel-horse of democracy, Walt Whitman. In one of his lectures, Whitman says:

Before the American era, the programme of the classes read thus, first
the king, second the noblemen and the gentry, third the great mass of
mechanics, farmers, men following the water, and all laboring persons.
The first and second classes are unknown to the theory of the government

---

[10] Barrett Wendell, *A Literary History of America* (New York, 1900), p. 353.

[11] Beecher's preaching to the common people is mentioned by Oliver Wendell
Holmes, *Life and Letters of Oliver Wendell Holmes* (Boston, 1896), II, 209. "Here
is the most popular Protestant preacher, I think, that ever lived, a man whose
church would be filled, if there was a bull-fight in the next street,—who gets a
salary of twenty thousand dollars and is worth it to his church—who, as a lecturer, is handled by his impresario as if he were a prima donna—who has done
more sensible, effective, good-natured talking and writing to the great middle
class and the 'unknown public' than any man we ever had in this country."

of these States; the likes of the class rated third on the old programme were intended to be, and are, in fact, to all intents and purposes, the American nation, the people.[12]

This belief in the common people found expression in the poetry of the nineteenth century. Beecher praises Wordsworth and Cowper for delivering English literature from its disdain for the common people.[13] Wordsworth went to the common people for his subjects because he believed there was more human reality to be found there. He declared, "I have chosen subjects from common life, and endeavoured to bring my language near to the real language of men."[14] With this belief in the common people, Beecher was in hearty sympathy. It will be next to impossible to understand Beecher's principles of composition unless we realize that he aimed to reach the common people. Beecher's heroes were those who struggled for the rights of the people; he preferred Wendell Phillips to Choate; Sumner to Webster.

In urging young men to study life first-hand, Beecher did not exclude the possibility of their learning a great deal from books. How natural in his attempt to know about human motives that he should have turned to dramatic literature. His study of the drama is suggested in the following report of a conversation with Beecher by Dion Boucicault.[15] "He went on to enumerate the number of great men from Sophocles to

[12] C. J. Furness, "Address on the Eighteenth Presidency," *Walt Whitman's Workshop* (Harvard University Press, 1928), p. 85.

[13] Beecher says, "As late as the day of Cowper, English literature, from its day-dawn down through Dryden and Pope, and all that class of poets, was one that stung the under-classes with a perpetual contempt. Nothing was more despicable than this paganism of English literature, to the days of its deliverance at the hands of such poets as Cowper and Wordsworth." *A Treasury of Illustration* (New York, 1904), p. 523,

[14] *Preface to Lyrical Ballads.*

[15] Edward Bok, *Beecher Memorial* (New York, 1887), p. 39.

Shakespeare, nobles of the human race, that had been the children of the drama." Beecher told Lawrence Barrett[16] that the drama was one of the foremost literary influences of all ages. Edwin Booth,[17] although he never met Beecher, cherished a warm regard for him. We are told by Harriet Beecher Stowe[18] that her brother read the Elizabethan dramatists with a great deal of pleasure and profit. Ford, Massinger, Beaumont, and Fletcher, and Marlowe taught him much about the human heart, but Shakespeare[19] taught him vastly more. Beecher's reverence for the master playwright breathes through every word of his description of his visit to Stratford on Avon in 1850. Of Shakespeare's influence, he says, "Not once in an age, not once in a hundred ages is there a Paul. But such great natures disperse their powers in others, and live on. Not another Shakespeare; but, by reason of his having lived, a hundred poets have sung who would not have been inspired otherwise."[20] During a luncheon together, Ellen Terry[21] and Henry Irving were surprised and pleased to hear Beecher recite long passages from Shakespeare; both declared that he might have made a great Shakespearean actor.

A few of the many authors who found a place on his library shelves were Plato and Homer; Dante, whose *Divine Comedy* and Milton's *Paradise Lost* were compared by the youthful Beecher at Amherst College; Bunyan and George Crabbe, whose sympathy for the common people appealed to him; Drummond and Giles Fletcher were favorites; Daniel, whose

[16] *Ibid.*, p. 22.   [17] *Ibid.*, p. 8.

[18] Harriet Beecher Stowe, *Men of Our Times* (Hartford, Conn., 1868), p. 530.

[19] Beecher owned eight editions of Shakespeare's works, besides various other critical works on Shakespeare. *Auction Sale Catalogue* (New York, 1887), pp. 181–82.

[20] *Treasury of Illustration* (New York, 1904), p. 519.

[21] Ellen Terry, *The Story of My Life* (London, 1913), p. 291.

poem "To Lady Margaret" was a shaping influence on his life; Burke, whose complete works were purchased with the first ten dollars earned while lecturing as a student at Amherst College; Walter Scott, whom he evidently tried to emulate in his novel *Norwood;* Ruskin, of whom he said, "I owe more to Ruskin than to any theologian."[22] Then there were Dickens, Thackeray, George Eliot, Sterne, Swift, Coleridge, and Keats (Beecher speaks of sucking the honey out of Keats). Others were Gladstone, Darwin, Herbert Spencer, Bain, Goethe, Kant, Rousseau, Renan, Schiller, Ribot, J. S. Mill, Longfellow, Whittier, O. W. Holmes, Lowell, Froude, Matthew Arnold, De Tocqueville, Calvin, Jeremy Taylor, Jonathan Edwards, J. H. Newman, George Campbell, Robert Dale—but the list goes on indefinitely. W. S. Searle,[23] Beecher's personal physician, estimated that Beecher had a library of fifteen thousand books. Fortunately, the *Auction Sale Catalogue*[24] preserves for us the titles and authors of most of the books on Beecher's shelves. Beecher was an omnivorous reader. His interest carried him into science as well as into the drama, into poetry as well as into philosophy, into criticism as well as into the field of biblical literature. Of libraries and books he has much to say. "Few places affected me," he declared, "more than libraries and especially the Bodleian library, reputed to have half a million printed books and manuscripts."[25]

It is of special interest to us in our study of Beecher's rhetorical theory that his study of rhetoric and belles letters amounted to a passion with him. Although Beecher did not distinguish himself as a student in most of the branches of

[22] *Yale Lectures*, third series, p. 108.

[23] W. S. Searle, "Personality of Henry Ward Beecher," *North American Review*, XLCIV, 487.

[24] *Auction Sale Catalogue* (New York, 1887).

[25] *Star Papers* (New York, 1855), p. 53.

learning at Amherst College, he did make a name for himself in debating. He was the best debater in his college generation.[26] He urged his listeners at Yale College to develop their ability to speak. Of his own development, he said, "I practised public speaking from the time of my sophomore year in college."[27] The college catalogues covering the years of his residence at Amherst College list the following books on rhetoric which were required of all students of rhetoric. We may assume that Beecher studied them, for rhetoric, as I have formerly shown, was his favorite study.[28] These texts were S. B. Newman, *Practical System of Rhetoric*,[29] George Campbell, *Philosophy of Rhetoric*, Whately, *Elements of Rhetoric*, and Blair, *Lectures on*

[26] Roswell D. Hitchcock, son of the then president, and college contemporary of Beecher at Amherst College, describes Beecher's interest at Amherst College: "It is idle to inquire what he might have accomplished in the more exact and severer studies of the college curriculum, had he been compelled, or persuaded to do his best in them. Mathematics he disliked and neglected. In the auction then usual at the end of the college course, Beecher's copy of 'Conic Sections' was put up as a 'clean copy, with leaves uncut.' Of Greek and Latin, as afterward of Hebrew, he probably never tried to know much. He cared little for the niceties of linguistic scholarship. Comparative philology might have interested him had his studies led him in that direction. As it was, he cared more for comparative anatomy than for comparative philology. Political economy would no doubt have been a favorite study, had it then occupied the position it now does. Butler's 'Analogy' was probably the most thoroughly mastered of all his textbooks. He was far enough from being indolent, but he never worked methodically. His reading took a wide range, and he had a quick and easy way of getting what he wanted out of a book. His forte was oratory, and decidedly the oratory of improvisation. He could think, and think best perhaps upon his feet. Storm and contradiction only made him more brilliant and forceful. He was, by all odds, the best debater of his college generation."—*Beecher Memorial* (New York, 1887), pp. 71–72.

[27] *Yale Lectures* (1st ser.), p. 143.

[28] Cf. W. S. Tyler, *History of Amherst* (Springfield, Mass., 1873), p. 515.

[29] This text is not as well known today as those of Blair, Campbell, and Whately. Newman borrows heavily from Blair and Campbell. The book evinces a thorough acquaintance with the ancient rhetoricians.

Rhetoric, and Belles Lettres.[30] In the *Auction Sale Catalogue* many volumes of Cicero's orations are cited.[31] Dialogues upon the *Character of the Orator*, and other like items appear in the list. Demosthenes' orations[32] are also included.

In addition to these words, which suggest Beecher's reading along the lines of rhetoric, Herbert Spencer's *Philosophy of Style* should be mentioned.

I think a young man might read for style profitably; but, after all, reading for style has a very limited function after a man gets ideas. The best essay on style that I know is that by Herbert Spencer; and every young man ought to get it, read it and practice it. He says, that is the best style which takes the thought or feeling or fancy of the speaker, and has the power of reproducing it on the retina of another person's mind. Though the manner and the moods of doing this may vary in detail, there are certain great fixed principles which do not vary. First among these, Herbert Spencer places this: that it is to be done with the least possible labor to the person receiving the idea; and in this respect he is directly opposed to Coleridge, who puts forward the theory that a man who has to dig for knowledge gets more benefit than one who acquires it without the trouble of digging.[33]

As the thesis progresses I shall point out evidences of the influence of Herbert Spencer's theory of "economy" on Beecher's rhetorical theory.

We must remember, too, in our consideration of Beecher's rhetorical training that he was reared to the ministry. Lyman Beecher, who was one of the most distinguished divines in New England during his generation, and, who, in 1831, became president of the then flourishing Lane Seminary in the great frontier metropolis, Cincinnati, without question gave invaluable lessons to his son on the theory of preaching. Probably his

[30] Cf. Amherst College *Catalogues*, 1830–31; 1831–32; 1832–33; 1833–34.

[31] *Auction Sale Catalogue* (New York, 1887), p. 62.   [32] *Ibid.*, p. 73.

[33] Henry Ward Beecher, "Plans for Home Reading," *Hints for Home Reading* (New York, 1880), p. 53, Lyman Abbott (ed.).

father turned his attention to the masters of pulpit oratory. In his acquisition of rhetorical skill, Beecher found help in the sermons of South, Barrow, Howe, Sherlock, Butler, and Edwards.

I was a great reader of the old sermonizers. I read old Robert South through and through; I saturated myself with South; I formed much of my style and my handling of texts on his methods. I obtained a vast amount of instruction and assistance from others of those old sermonizers, who were as familiar to me as my own name. I read Barrow, Howe, Sherlock, Butler, Edwards, particularly. I preached a great many sermons while reading these old men, and upon their discourses I often founded the framework of my own. After I had preached them I said to myself, "That will never do; I wouldn't preach that way again for all the world."[34]

In the list of preachers just given, the name of Edwards refers to Jonathan Edwards, America's first great philosopher-theologian. In another connection Beecher has more to say of his debt to Edwards in the matter of sermon construction.

No man can inherit experience. It must be born in each man for himself. After the light dawned, I could then see how plainly Jonathan Edwards's sermons were so made. Those gigantic *applications* of his were only the stretching out of the arms of the sermon upon the hearts and lives of his audience. I could see it now, and wondered that I had not seen it before. But having caught the idea, I went eagerly through Edwards to see how he took aim. I found his sermons to be either a statement and establishment of a plain principle, or an exceedingly abundant collection of Scriptural teachings around some great central truth. This was not, however, the sermon; it was only a battery thrown up. Then from these bulwarks and batteries came a fire upon the life, the hearts, the character, the conduct, of living men, just as they lived in Edwards's days, such as I think no uninspired man ever surpassed, if any ever equalled it. It was a kind of moral inquisition, and sinners were put upon the argumentative racks, and beneath screws, and, with an awful revolution of the great truth in hand, evenly and steadily screwed down and crushed. I never could read that sermon, 'Sinner in the hands of an angry God,' at one

[34] *Yale Lectures* (1st ser.), p. 146.

sitting. I think a person of moral sensibility alone at midnight, reading that awful discourse, would well nigh go crazy. He would hear the judgment-trump, and see the advancing heaven, and the day of doom would begin to mantle him with its shroud.

But we have wandered—not exactly wandered either—for the book of the Acts of the Apostles and Edwards's Sermons were the two masters at whose feet we sat while learning that preaching is only another name for taking hold of men and moulding them.[35]

Later in our discussion of Beecher's theory of sermon planning we will take up the matter of the rhetorical influence of Jonathan Edwards mentioned in the above quotation. From these various sources Beecher acquired information that would assist him in developing his own rhetorical theory.

Beecher's study of the psychology of persuasion led him very naturally into an inquiry of mental philosophy. His lifelong interest in physiological psychology had its inception at Amherst College. His sister, Mrs. Stowe, writes:

Mr. Beecher and his associates formed a club for physiological research. He himself immediately started reading right and left, in all the works of anatomy and physiology which he could lay his hands on, either in the college or village libraries. He sent and bought for his own private use, Magendie's *Physiology*, Combe's *Phrenology*, and the works of Gall and Spurzheim. A phrenological union was formed to purchase together charts, models and dissecting tools, for the study of comparative anatomy. It was even planned in the enthusiasm of young discipleship to establish a private dissecting room for the club, but the difficulties attending the procuring of proper subjects prevented its being carried into effect. He may be said during his college course to have constructed for himself a physiological mental philosophy out of the writings of the Scotch metaphysical school of Combe, Spurzheim, and the other physiologists.[36]

A study of psychology yields much of value to the preacher. Besides studying his own mental processes, Beecher studied the mental traits and habits of those around him, individually and

[35] Henry Ward Beecher, *Eyes and Ears* (New York, 1862), pp. 111–12.

[36] *Men of Our Times*, pp. 529–30.

in the aggregate. Small wonder that Beecher's interest in the workings of the human mind carried him into a study of phrenology, especially when we recall that Fowler was his roommate at college. Our respect for Beecher's intelligence and sincerity is saved, however, when we realize that Herbert Spencer was once attracted to this then new study. Then, too, Beecher was more interested in the physiological aspects of phrenology than in its treatment of the physical manifestations of character. Beecher's interest in the study of man led him to the works of Alexander Bain and Herbert Spencer.[37]

In the first place you must study facts, scientifically. I think that such works as Bain's while criticisable in many directions are nevertheless works of great interest as showing a wise tendency in the investigation of the mind of man,—the founding of mental philosophy upon physiology. I do not commend the system in all its particulars, but I speak of its tendency in the right direction. I would say the same, also, of Herbert Spencer's works. There is much in him that I believe will be found sovereign and noble in the final account of truth, when our knowledge of it is rounded up. The direction he is moving in is a wise one, which is the study of human nature, of the totality of man.[38]

This statement was made in the *Yale Lectures* in 1872, and it gives us a clue as to Beecher's reading along scientific lines. In Dr. Duncan's *Life and Letters of Herbert Spencer* there are several interesting references to Henry Ward Beecher. Beecher[39] was the author of the note to Herbert Spencer accompanying a sum of subscription money. Some of the other Americans subscribing to the support of Herbert Spencer's work were

[37] Alexander Bain's *The Sense and Intellect* was first published in 1855. It is interesting to note in passing that Alexander Bain, then Lord Rector of the University of Aberdeen, was present at Beecher's lecture in that city in September, 1886: *A Summer in England with Henry Ward Beecher* (New York, 1887), p. 63; Herbert Spencer's *Principles of Psychology* was published also in 1855.

[38] *Yale Lectures* (1st ser.), p. 90.

[39] Dr. David Duncan, *The Life and Letters of Herbert Spencer* (London, 1908), p. 128.

Henry W. Bellows, Edward Everett, Dr. Furness, James Russell Lowell, and Oliver Wendell Holmes. Spencer[40] refers in a friendly fashion to Beecher and his preaching on the doctrine of evolution. At a dinner in 1882, given in honor of Herbert Spencer on the occasion of his visit to America, at which Beecher was one of the chief speakers, Beecher paid this tribute to the influence of Herbert Spencer upon him. "To my father and mother I owe my physical being; to you sir, I owe my intellectual being. At a critical moment you provided the safe paths through the bogs and morasses; you were my teacher."[41] In his popular lecture entitled "Evolution and Religion," Beecher quoted Herbert Spencer's[42] definition of evolution. It is an interesting fact, for it shows Beecher's concern with science, that the works of Spencer, Tyndall and Huxley were published in this country largely through the influence of Beecher.

Beecher's interest in the study of physical nature led him to Gray's *Structural Botany.* Loudon's works, his encyclopedias of horticulture and of agriculture, were studied by Beecher

---

[40] *Ibid.*, p. 252.

[41] Dr. William A. Hammond, who sat beside Beecher during this dinner, remarked, "I shall never forget the effect of his ringing words upon the audience, composed as it was mainly of hard-headed men who were not accustomed to be swayed by their emotions. They rose to their feet, waved their table-napkins, and shouted themselves hoarse, not because they all approved of the views which he then revealed to them but because of the astounding courage, the wonderful regard for the truth as he understood it, and the almost superhuman honesty by which he must have been actuated." Quoted by Newell Dwight Hillis, *Lectures and Orations of Henry Ward Beecher* (New York, 1912), p. 313.

[42] *The Auction Catalogue* (New York, 1887), contains the following books by Spencer; Works, 14 vols. (London, 1868–71); Essays (London, 1858), Essays (New York, 1866); *Principles of Psychology* (London, 1855); *Ecclesiastical Institutions* (London, 1885), presentation copy from the author; *Education* (New York, 1861); *First Principles of Philosophy* (New York, 1865). In addition to these there are such critical volumes as W. Ground's *An Examination of the Structural Principles of Mr. Herbert Spencer's Philosophy* (Oxford, 1883), and M. Guthrie's *On Mr. Spencer's Unification of Knowledge* (London, 1882).

during his years at Indianapolis. While in Indiana Beecher edited a magazine devoted to the growing of fruits and flowers.
Beecher held that the preacher should know nature from first-
hand experience. No one knew better than Beecher what
hosts of illustrations could be drawn from a knowledge of
nature.

> You ought to know the gardener's thoughts, his ambitions and feelings.
> You ought to know what is done in the barn, in the cellar, in the vine-
> yard, and everywhere. You ought to know and understand a naturalist's
> enthusiasm when he finds a new flower or a new bug—that ecstasy is
> almost like a heaven of heavens to the apocalyptic John.[43]

At Indianapolis, Beecher took the three first prizes for the best
exhibition of squashes, beets, and oyster-plants.[44] His summer
home at Peekskill on the Hudson, Boscobel, upon which he
lavished so much of his earnings, boasted a variety of trees
second only to the arboretum of one of our national institutions.[45] His summers, when the seasons permitted, his Mon-
days during the rest of the year, were spent on his farm super-
vising the planting and harvesting of crops, observing the laws
of nature.[46] All this while he was in the homiletic mood. His

[43] *Yale Lectures* (1st ser.), p. 171.

[44] W. C. Beecher and S. Scoville, and Mrs. H. W. Beecher, *Life and Letters
of Henry Ward Beecher* (New York, 1888), p. 199.

[45] Beecher thus describes his debt to nature: "I would not for all the comfort
which I might get from the books of the Alexandrian Library, or from the Lenox
Library, give up the comfort which I get out of nature. Nature, now that I have
had the revelation of God which interprets it to me, I would not give up for
anything. I had almost said that I would rather lose my Bible than to lose my
world." *Yale Lectures* (3d ser.), p. 107.

[46] On Beecher's intimacy with nature, John Burroughs remarks, "I owe Mr.
Beecher a debt as a student of nature. My first acquaintance with his mind was
through his 'Star Papers,' a volume which came into my hands one summer day
in 1857. It shows him mainly as a writer upon nature and rural themes, in which
field his heartiness, his boyishness, his flowing animal spirits, his love of beauty,
his lively fancy, and above all his solvent power of emotion and imagination
which enabled him to transmute and spiritualize natural objects had full swing."
Beecher Memorial, pp. 93, 94.

sermons reflect his passion for nature; spiritual laws are strikingly illustrated by natural phenomena.

It was only a step from the beautiful in nature to the beautiful in art. His library contained books on architecture, painting, sculpture, engraving, etching, music, organ-building, cosmetics, pottery, porcelains, flowers, trees, etc. Beecher's taste led him to purchase among other works of art, choice editions of Hogarth's works, the very rare *Holy Land*, by Roberts, the plates of which, by special contract, were destroyed after the limited edition had been printed. Among the other collections on his shelves were *Musée Française*, Foster's *British Gallery*, a large folio copy of Lodge's *Portraits*, very sumptuous works on uncut India paper, with artist's proofs, superb works on foreign cathedrals, *Galerie de Florence*, and the *Beauties of the Court of Charles II*. Beecher owed much of his interest in painting to his visit to the galleries of the Louvre and Luxembourg, when his congregation sent him to Europe in 1850.[47]

Beecher held that God is often revealed to individuals through their sense of the beautiful. Men and women can often be persuaded to a better way of living through their aesthetic sense.

There are minds that open to spiritual things through the artistic side of their nature more readily and easily than through any other. This should be recognized. When I entered the first gallery of any magnitude in Europe, it was a revelation to me; I was deeply affected. It was at the

[47] "Thence to the Palace de Luxembourg. But here there is a gallery of paintings! Ah, what a new world has been opened to me! What a new sense within myself. . . . . To find myself absolutely intoxicated—to find my system so affected that I could not control my nerves—to find myself trembling and laughing and weeping, and almost hysterical, and that in spite of my shame and resolute endeavor to behave better—such a power of these galleries over me I had not expected. I have lived for two days in a fairy-land." "Experiences of Art and Nature," *Star Papers* (New York, 1855), p. 56. An idea of Beecher's interest in engravings, etchings, drawings, paintings, porcelains, and fine rugs can be gathered from a study of the *Auction Sale Catalogue* (New York, 1887). For example, there are 786 entries in the catalogue of line engravings and etchings.

Luxembourg. I had never imagined such a wealth of glory. The sense of exhilaration was so transcendent that I felt as if I could not stay in the body. I was filled with that supersensitiveness of supernal feeling which is true worship; and I never seemed to myself so near the gate of heaven. I never felt capable of so nearly understanding my Master; never in all my life was I so conscious of such an earnestness to do his work, and to do it better than I did, as while under the all-pervading influence of that gallery of beauty.[48]

During his second lecture tour of the United States, Charles Dickens[49] lectured in Plymouth Church. In a letter describing his meeting with Beecher he reported that Beecher had a good knowledge of art.

So far I have attempted to show the nature and extent of Beecher's interests. To preach in such a pulpit for forty years necessitated vast accumulations of knowledge. The Plymouth Church pulpit was always in need of new materials. Its insatiable appetite sent Beecher foraging into all the realms of human activity for pabulum. Like Dickens, or any other author, Beecher was forever making notes for future reference. Keenly did he observe human life; eagerly did he pore over books, and most carefully did he study how to enter into the hearts of his fellow-men. One of his activities which was important as a source of materials was his lecturing.[50] His lecture-tours with J. B. Pond, who managed Beecher as he would a prima donna, as Oliver Wendell Holmes said, took them all over the United States and England; they traveled more than 300,000 miles throughout the United States, and sailed the

[48] *Yale Lectures* (1st ser.), p. 57.

[49] John Forster, *Life of Dickens* (Philadelphia, 1872), III, 416.

[50] Regarding Beecher's ability on the platform, we have this testimony from Mark Twain, "Beecher, Gough, Nasby and Anna Dickenson were the only lecturers who knew their own value and exacted it. In towns their fee was $200.00 and $250.00, in cities $400.00. The lyceum always got a profit out of these four (weather permitting) but generally lost again on the house emptiers." *Autobiography* (New York, 1924), I, 157.

Atlantic three times. One can be sure that these peregrinations yielded much in the way of sermon materials. The frequent visits into the interior of the United States helped Beecher to learn the temper of the times; they helped him to become a political prognosticator of importance. From his railroad companions he gathered many ideas; he learned about human nature direct. Always on these journeys he carried a black bag filled with books which occupied his attention when no travelers offered talk. Much of his reading was done on the trains. His chief book was the Bible. He studied this book as he studied no other, particularly the New Testament. Books of a scientific nature, books relating to evolution, books on higher criticism, books on art—all these and others found their way into the black bag. Beecher's mental reservoir was continually receiving impressions to be poured out later as occasion demanded. Beecher's vast resources caused Abraham Lincoln to say to Theodore Cuyler, "The most marvelous thing about Mr. Beecher is his inexhaustible fertility."[51]

B

We have viewed the diverse avenues over which multitudinous ideas came trooping into Beecher's subconscious mind.[52] It will be interesting to investigate now what happened to these impressions which were later to emerge as parts of unified

[51] Theodore L. Cuyler, *Recollections of a Long Life* (New York, 1902), p. 215.

[52] John Galsworthy (in *The Creation of Character in Literature* [Oxford University Press, 1931], p. 5), has described the literary worker's subconscious mind. "In the human being these impacts are so infinitely many we seem each of us to be a complete reservoir of subconscious experience, a secret storehouse of first-hand contacts, sights, sounds, scents, tastes, and of impressions at second-hand. If one can imagine the Catacombs at Rome, or the old cellars under the Adelphi, stored to the brim with photographic film, one has perhaps some notion of what the human subconscious is like. Every minute, every second indeed of our existence adds to recorded experience stocked and piled to be drawn upon."

discourses. Thoughts from Milton,[53] observations from the Louvre, illustrations from the building of the Brooklyn bridge, and lessons learned from raising beets could hardly be presented to an audience without some sort of fusion taking place. This process of welding one idea with another, forming new concepts capable of being transmitted to others, Beecher termed the imagination and designated it "the most important of all the elements that go to make the preacher."

In describing how he created a concept of God, Beecher is giving in outline his theory of the imaginative process. I take it that the following account is an evidence of how he believed the creative process worked; not only are concepts of God formed in this way but sermons are also thus created.

The first element on which your preaching will largely depend for power and success, you will perhaps be surprised to learn, is the Imagination, which I regard as the most important of the elements that go to make up the preacher. Imagination is indispensable to the formation of any clear and distinct ideas of God, the Father, the Son, or the Holy Ghost. For myself I am compelled to say that I must form an ideal of God through his son Jesus Christ; Christ is Indispensable to me. My nature needs to fashion the thought of God, though I know him to be a

[53] I mention Milton here because Beecher was extraordinarily fond of his writings. He once said: "If I were to read this week in some of the nobler writings of John Milton, you would hear the trumpet sounding next Sunday in Plymouth Church" (*Hints on Home Reading* [New York, 1880], p. 54). The *Auction Sale Catalogue* lists the following of John Milton's Works: *Works in Verse and Prose, From the Original Editions, With Life of the Author*, by the Rev. John Mitford, Portrait, 8 vols., 8vo, full morocco antique, gilt edges (London, Pickering, 1851); *Works in Prose and Verse;* Notes, etc., by John Mitford, 4 vols., royal 8vo, cloth, Large paper copy (Philadelphia, 1864); *Poetical Works*, with *Memoir, and Critical Remarks*, by James Montgomery, 120 engravings on wood, from drawings by William Harvey, 2 vols., 8vo, morocco, gilt (London, 1843); *Poetical Works, With Notes and Life*, Portrait, 2 vols., 8vo, boards (Boston, 1834); *Paradise Lost*, Edited by Thomas Newton, Baskerville Edition, Royal 8vo, calf, gilt (Birmingham, 1760); *Milton's Paradise Lost*, Illustrated by Gustave Dore, with Notes and Life of Milton by Robert Vaughan, 4to, cloth gilt, gilt edges (New York, 1885).

spirit, into something that shall nearly or remotely represent that which I know. I hold before my mind, therefore, a glorified form; but after all the glory, whatever may be the nimbus and the effluence[54] around about it, it is to me the form of a glorified man. And, therefore, I fashion to myself out of the spirit, that which has to me, as it were, a Divine presence and a Divine being, namely, a Divine man. Imagination is the power to bring from the depths the things that are hidden from the bodily eye. Imagination is the true germ of faith; it is the power of conceiving as definite things which are invisible to the senses,—of giving them distinct shape. And this not merely in your own thoughts, but with the power of representing the things which experience cannot primarily teach to other people's minds, so that they shall be just as obvious as though seen with the bodily eye.[55]

From this quotation, we see that Beecher believed that experience is the basis of the creative process. The new concept must, in his own words, represent "that which I know." The concept of God is formed from his knowledge of Jesus Christ gathered from a study of the New Testament, and from his accumulated insight into the best traits of mankind. This partially neo-classic and partially romantic conception of the imaginative process Beecher most likely received from his study of S. P. Newman's[56] *Practical System of Rhetoric*. Cice-

[54] It is interesting to compare Beecher's phraseology *nimbus* and *effluence* with that of William James, *Principles of Psychology* (New York, 1899), I, 255. "The significance, the value, of the image is all in his *halo* or *penumbra* that surrounds and escorts it—or rather that is fused into one with it and has become bone of its bone and flesh of its flesh."

[55] *Yale Lectures* (1st ser.), p. 111; Beecher mentions the importance of the imagination also on p. 8 and p. 240, of the *Yale Lectures* (1st ser.); and in the *Treasury of Illustration*, the importance of the imagination is treated in sections 379, 1976, and 2326. Nothing, however, is added in these places that does not appear in the above quotation. See also *Yale Lectures* (3d ser.), pp. 121 and 305.

[56] S. P. Newman, *Practical System of Rhetoric* (New York, 1834), p. 55. "To show in what way taste guides the artist in designing his work, I shall here introduce an account given by Cicero of the course pursued by Zeuxis, when employed by the Crotonians to paint the picture of a beautiful female. The city of Crotona was celebrated for the beauty of its females. Zeuxis requested, that those esteemed most beautiful might be assembled at the same place. From these he

ro's[57] account of Zeuxis and the painting of the beautiful maiden of Crotona is repeated by Newman. It will be recalled that Zeuxis formed his ideal conception of a beautiful female after he had viewed five of the most beautiful virgins in Crotona. Beecher's idealization of man was a similar process. We discern, also, in the phrase, "I fashion to myself," that Beecher recognized the synthetic phase of the imaginative process acting under the impulse of the will. The process was under partial control. He selected the best traits to make up his composite picture of God as did Zeuxis in his picture. In the phrase of "Giving them distinct shape . . . . with the power of representing things to other people's minds," Beecher recognized the unification phase of the imaginative process, and the necessity of transmitting the result to others.[58] These three

---

selected five, who in his estimation excelled all the others in beauty, and by combining in his picture the most striking traits of beauty in each of these five, he executed the task assigned to him. Now in the whole process, taste was evidently the guide of the artist. The selection of the five most beautiful virgins, the choice of the most beautiful traits in each, are both instances of judgment, founded on the experience of past emotions. But this is only the preparation for his work. What has been thus selected must now be combined together and so combined as to produce one harmonious effect. Instead of an assemblage of beautiful limbs and features, an air and proportion must be given to the form, and a cast to the countenance. Here is exercise for the designing powers of the artist, and over this part of the work also taste must preside. Different modes of combination present themselves before the 'mind's eye,' and of these different combinations, one is to be selected as most beautiful. The making of this selection is evidently an instance of judgment, founded on the experience of past emotions of beauty. Zeuxis was familiar with forms of beauty, and had fixed in his mind those principles of judging, which enabled him to decide with readiness and correctness. Hence, no doubt, his celebrity as a painter of the female form."

[57] Cicero, *De inventione* (London, 1760), Book II.

[58] Wordsworth expresses the necessity of transmitting the new concept to others:

> "A new world—a world, too, that is fit
> To be transmitted, and to other eyes
> Made visible; as ruled by those fixed laws
> Whence spiritual dignity originates,

[Footnote continued on following page]

phases[59] are experience, synthesis of ideas,[60] and the creation of a new concept capable of being transmitted to others.

Fortunately, the above quoted paragraph is not the only instance of Beecher's consideration of his practice of the creative process. Scattered here and there in his works are suggestions which shed further light upon his insight into the problems of literary creation. These suggestions concern his preparation, his synthetic process, and his act of speaking.

Beecher would not preach upon a theme that had not engaged his attention for a long time. He prepared the man rather than the particular message. "My whole life," he says, "is a general preparation."[61] We have seen how he went here and there over the highways and byways of life gathering material,

> Which do both give it being and maintain
> A balance, an ennobling interchange
> Of action, from without and from within
> The excellence, pure function, and best power
> Both of the objects seen, and the eye that sees."
> —*The Prelude* (ed. E. De Selincourt), Book XIII, vss. 368–78

[59] These three phases are given by Professor C. Spearman, *Creative Mind* (New York, 1931), chap. iii. He calls them the "Principle of Experience," the "Principle of Relations," the "Principle of Correlates." These three phases of the creative process are represented by Professor John Livingston Lowes (*The Road to Xanadu* [New York, 1927], p. 432), as the Well, the Will, and the Vision.

[60] A splendid description of Beecher composing in the presence of the audience is given by Charles Dudley Warner, "I heard him deliver once one of the foundation discourses on preaching to the theological students at Yale. It was an address of very considerable power, suggestive, reminiscent, witty, full of the wisdom of experience; but the great intellectual display came afterward, when he said that he would try to answer any questions put to him. . . . . His replies were always brief, and they came as quick as a flash of lightning. I never saw before or since—for it seemed as if you could see his mind flash—such an intellectual display. . . . . As he stood there all aglow, turning quickly from side to side, perfectly calm and yet nervously alive from his head to his feet, a curious smile wreathing his lips, and his eyes flaming and dancing, I thought I had never seen such a complete fusion of the physical and intellectual man. *Beecher Memorial* (New York, 1887), pp. 74–75.

[61] *Address to Students. A Summer in England with Henry Ward Beecher* (New York, 1886), p. 102.

never knowing when he was going to use the particular bit of information he was gleaning. There is a striking bit of testimony as to Beecher's preparation of the *Yale Lectures on Preaching* which is of significance to us in our consideration of his creative activity. Lyman Abbott records this conversation with Beecher. "When next I met him," Abbott relates, "I asked him, 'Where is that sermon on pulpit dynamics?' 'It is not ripe,' he replied; 'but I shall get something out of it yet.' What he did get out of it was, ten years later, the *Yale Lectures on Preaching*, one of the best pieces of work he ever did."[62] Observations collected with patient labor during his preaching career went into the making of these volumes.

There are many other evidences of Beecher's use of the ripening process. "The Background of Mystery"[63] (1877), a sermon, contains an illustration which he invented forty years previously as a youth at Mount Pleasant Academy.[64] In the *Star Papers* (1859) there is an essay on the psychology of the audience which is repeated in a modified version in the *Yale Lectures on Preaching* (1872). The composition of the "Liverpool Address" (1863) is the fusion of thoughts on slavery accumulated through the years. Beecher first came face to face with the evils of slavery in Cincinnati in 1836 when he patrolled the streets with a musket to defend the poor blacks, during the Birney riots. The thought that slavery was economically detrimental was no sudden whim or passing fancy with Beecher. In November, 1862, he employs the following analogy:

When a man is a savage, he has but one or two faculties to feed; but when he becomes civilized, he has a great many more mouths open calling for food. For the more the human mind is developed, the more numerous

[62] Lyman Abbott, *The Life of Henry Ward Beecher* (New York, 1904), p. 120.

[63] *Evolution and Religion* (New York, 1885), p. 151.

[64] *Patriotic Addresses* (ed. John R. Howard) (Boston, 1887), p. 29.

are its wants which must be supplied. And blessed is that nation which
is to supply the wants of a civilized people. They are great consumers.[65]

The thought here expressed finds expression in the "Liverpool
Address" in a different and more apt figure.

A savage is a man of one story, and that one story a cellar. When a
man begins to be civilized, he raises another story. When you Christianize
and civilize the man, you put story upon story, for you develop faculty
after faculty; and you have to supply every story with your productions.
The savage is a man one story deep; the civilized man is thirty stories
deep.[66]

Other speakers have depended upon lifelong preparation for
their speeches. Whipple[67] records that the celebrated image of
the "British drum-beat" used so effectively by Webster in his
speech on *President Jackson's Protest* occurred to him years
before while in Quebec. Coleridge in describing his preparation for lecturing stressed the necessity of the ripening process.

I would not lecture on any subject for which I had to acquire the main
knowledge, even though a month or three months previous time were
allowed me; on no subject that had not employed my thoughts for a large
portion of my life since earliest manhood, free of all outward and particular purpose.[68]

The necessity for prolonged thought in the creative process is
emphasized by Wordsworth as a prerequisite for spontaneity
of utterance. The following quotation is especially pertinent
in our discussion of Beecher's creative process because, he, too,
believed that the unification of ideas should be spontaneous.
I shall discuss this matter of spontaneity again shortly.

All good poetry is the spontaneous overflow of powerful feelings; and
though this be true, poems, to which any value can be attached were
never produced on any variety of subjects but by a man who, being pos-

[65] *Ibid.*, "The Ground and Forms of Government," p. 401.

[66] *Ibid.*, "The Liverpool Address," p. 523.

[67] E. P. Whipple, "Daniel Webster as a Master of English Style," *The Great
Speeches and Orations of Daniel Webster* (Boston, 1882), p. xxviii.

[68] *Literary Remains* (ed. Shedd), II, 2, Letter to J. Britton, Esq.

sessed of more than usual organic sensibility, had also thought long and deeply.[69]

Beecher's practice of lifelong preparation permitted mastery of the subject. The subject could be looked at in all its relations. A process of subconscious cerebration wore off the sharpness of the original idea and integrated one thought with another. This process of subconscious cerebration is well expressed by Oliver Wendell Holmes:

Put an idea into your intelligence and leave it there an hour, a day, a year, without ever having occasion to refer to it. When at last you return to it, you do not find it as it was when acquired. It has domiciliated itself, so to speak, become at home, entered into relations with your own thoughts and integrated itself with the whole fabric of your mind.[70]

Periodically Beecher had to draw up from the subconscious materials for his sermons. During the week he brooded over the themes that he wanted to use the coming Sunday. His lifelong preparation provided the materials for his period of brooding. This is the first partially controlled stage of the creative process.

I know what I am going to aim at, but, of course, I don't get down to anything specific. I brood it, and ponder it, and dream over it, and pick up information about one point and another, but if I ever think I see the plan opening up to me I don't dare to look at it or put it down on paper. If once I write a thing out, it is almost impossible for me to kindle to it again. I never dare, nowadays, to write out a sermon during the week; that is sure to kill it. I have to think around and about it, get it generally ready, and *fuse*[71] it when the time comes.[72]

[69] *Preface to Lyrical Ballads.*

[70] *Autocrat of the Breakfast Table* (Boston, 1858), p. 134.

[71] Beecher's use of the word *fuse* is similar to Coleridge's employment of the word in his description of the creative imagination. *Biographia Literaria* (Shawcross edition [Oxford University Press, 1907]), chap. xiv, p. 12. "He diffuses a tone and spirit of unity, that blends, and (as it were) *fuses* each into each, by that synthetic and magical power, to which we have exclusively appropriated the name of imagination."

[72] Lyman Abbott and S. B. Halliday, *Henry Ward Beecher, A Sketch of His Career* (Hartford, Conn., 1887), p. 211.

Beecher was careful not to allow the process of fusion to take place anywhere except in the presence of the audience. He had learned to woo the creative muse. Emerson[73] has observed that all orators have "habits of heat" and that they take great pains to husband these periods of creative activity. To allow the theme to shape itself prematurely would kill inspiration when Beecher stood in the presence of the audience. His courting of the muse reminds one of a line from Keats:[74]

> The unchariest muse
> To embracements warm as theirs makes warm excuse.

Beecher wanted the chary muse to throw her mantle over his shoulder as he stood in the presence of his congregation on Sunday. Coleridge similarly brooded over his material during the preceding days and created his lecture in the presence of his audience.[75]

Beecher[76] learned, through years of struggling, to understand his own creative temperament, to handle the creative muse with care. He uses the word *nowadays* with appreciation of those earlier years when he attempted to write out the sermon during the week. No matter what his preparation, he was forever forsaking the "beaten oil" and preaching upon another theme and doing it surprisingly well. He was filled with anxiety. He feared that he was on the way to superficiality.

[73] *Essay on Eloquence.*

[74] H. Buxton Forman, *The Poetical Works of John Keats* (Oxford University Press, 1929), vss. 532–33.

[75] I have already referred to the letter of J. Britton, Esq. found in *Literary Remains* (ed. Shedd), II, 2–5. The practice of Coleridge in lecturing is described in this letter. Coleridge said, "I faithfully employ the intervening days in collecting and digesting the materials. . . . . Before I had proceeded twenty minutes, I have been obliged to push the manuscript away, and give the subject a new turn. Nay this was so notorious that many of my auditors used to threaten me, when they saw any number of written papers on my desk, to steal them away, declaring they never felt so secure of a good lecture as when they perceived that I had not a single scrap of writing before me."

[76] Cf. *Yale Lectures* (1st ser.), p. 205.

Finally, he awoke to the fact that he had to take into account his own temperament and prepare in his own way. He found where his strength lay. For him, there could be no completing of the sermon during the week. The only formal preparation he allowed himself was in the hour just preceding the sermon.[77]

Outlining the sermon on Sunday mornings was the next partially controlled stage of Beecher's creative process. Of his practice of ushering his thoughts from the realm of the subconscious to the fringe of the conscious on Sunday mornings, he relates:

> I have a dozen or more topics lying loose in my mind through the week; I think of one or another as occasion may serve, anywhere, at home, in the street, in the horse-car. I rarely know what theme I shall use until Sunday morning. Then, after breakfast I go into my study as a man goes into his orchard; I feel among these themes as he feels among his apples, to find the ripest and best; the theme which seems most ripe I pluck; then I select my text, analyze my subject, prepare the outline and go into the pulpit to preach it while it is fresh.[78]

As I have already suggested, by holding back the process of "crystallization" until Sunday morning,[79] Beecher was able to

[77] Such a practice is fraught with many dangers, Beecher knew as well as anyone else. In his *Address to Students* (London, 1886), he advised the student to prepare carefully. "I think that in the earlier part of a man's ministry, if he is ever so qualified, it is a good thing to constrain a man's thoughts in a just mood of preparation and get the conception of a well-organized sermon; but after that is acquired, the larger the liberty is the more fruitful a man will be in his work." Dr. William Pierson Merrill, *The Freedom of the Preacher* (New York, 1922), p. 28, expresses the hazards of this sort of preparation for the average person. "The fact that Henry Ward Beecher found his sermons for Sunday evenings as he walked in his garden for a few minutes Sunday afternoons proves not that that is the ideal method, nor that all men would find their way to true freedom of expression by following his example, but that he was a rarely gifted soul. I have known men, who, seeking to be free by following Mr. Beecher's method, have simply succeeded in becoming slaves to their own slovenliness."

[78] Lyman Abbott, *Henry Ward Beecher* (New York, 1904), p. 118.

[79] It is interesting that sometimes the creative process never reached the

keep the theme in ferment right up to the time of preaching. He wanted the theme to lie fallow in his mind as long as possible. In the hour just preceding the sermon, he marked out broad paths for his thoughts to take while composing in the presence of the audience.

Beecher, in studying his creative process, recognized that the thoughts shaped themselves very suddenly.

> When the time comes for me to do anything, I do not know why it should be so except I am of that temperament—it crystallizes and very suddenly, too, and as much of it as I am going to use for that distinct time comes right up before my mind in full form, and I sketch it down and rely upon my facility, through long experience, to give utterance and full development to it after I come before an audience. There is nothing in this world that is such a stimulus to me as an audience; it wakes up the power of thinking and wakes up the power of the imagination in me.[80]

This was an important phase of his "habit of heat." He had schooled himself so that this process of sudden synthesis took place just before he went on the platform. The sudden nature of the creative process is suggested in those familiar lines of Wordsworth:

> They flash upon the inward eye
> Which is the bliss of solitude.[81]

Professor C. D. Thorpe speaks of the suddenness of the process of crystallization: "The aesthetic experience is a product of synthesis and fusion—a flashing together of mental atomies of

---

stage of passing from the subconscious to the conscious. Gestation never reached completion. When Beecher was in England in 1886, he was to have given an address on Burns; a bad cold prevented him from speaking. He told his lecture manager with much regret, "I believe one of the best speeches that was ever in me has never come out; it was for that Burns Centennial." *A Summer in England*, p. 65.

[80] *Address to Students*, p. 103; *op. cit.*, p. 29.

[81] *I Wandered Lonely as a Cloud*.

diverse origin and nature."[82] Throughout the week Beecher was
pointing toward this hour of special preparation when he welded his ideas into a harmonious whole.

Beecher's practice of employing so little formal preparation
is not peculiar to him. Spurgeon[83] was accustomed to spend an
hour on Saturday evenings in outlining his sermon for Sunday
morning. Phillips Brooks believed that the less of special preparation needed for a sermon, the better the sermon.

The subject chosen next will come the special preparation for the
sermon. This ought to consist in bringing together and arranging, and
illuminating a knowledge of the subject and thought about it which has
already been in the possession of the preacher. I think that the less of
special preparation that is needed for a sermon, the better the sermon is.
The best sermon would be that whose thoughts, though carefully arranged, and lighted up with every illustration that could make them
clearer for this special appearance, were all old thoughts, familiar to the
preacher's mind, long a part of his experience.[84]

Beecher allowed as little time as possible to elapse between
his special preparation and the time of speaking. His church
was hard by his residence. On entering the church he went directly to the pulpit, and very shortly was in the act of composing, of clothing the outline worked out in his study.[85] During
the opening moments he paid close attention to his outline but
as he kindled to his subject he paid less and less heed to his
prepared notes. He believed that no man could extemporize
until he had cut the cord that tied him to his notes. As he
composed in the presence of his congregation, he was in the
act of "bringing from the depths the things that are hidden

[82] C. D. Thorpe, "The Aesthetic Experience as Illumination," *Studies in
Honor of Fred Newton Scott* (University of Chicago Press, 1929), p. 211.

[83] W. Y. Fullerton, *C. H. Spurgeon*, A Biography (London, 1920), p. 217.

[84] Phillips Brooks, *Lectures on Preaching* (New York, 1877), p. 156.

[85] Sometimes Beecher abandoned the prepared sermon plan and preached upon
another subject. This phase of his preaching will be taken up in the chapter on
sermon organization.

from the bodily eye and giving them distinct shape so as to be capable of being understood by others."[86] The audience put Beecher in possession of all his faculties. "There are," he declared, "a thousand shades of thought reflected from the faces of the people." How similar this is to Hazlitt's remark, "The orator sees his subject in the eager looks of his audience."[87] For Beecher, the audience was the vitalizing factor in the production of a sermon. All his preparation culminated in the act of speaking. The whole creative process came to a head and burst forth under the inspiration of a congregation of three thousand people. Wordsworth's phrase, already referred to, "spontaneous overflow of powerful feelings," certainly applied to Beecher's preaching. The spontaneous character of effective preaching was expressed by Phillips Brooks in that picturesque sentence, "A sermon should be like the leaping of a fountain not the pumping of a pump."[88]

As I have said many times, the force behind the leaping-forth of the sermon came from years of acquisition of materials and thought. The period of gestation covered his entire mental life. During the week preceding the preaching of a particular sermon, he would draw up from the subconscious several possible themes. These he would turn over and over in his mind without allowing any one of them to take on definite shape.[89] On Sunday morning, he would decide which was the

[86] *Yale Lectures* (1st ser.), p. 111.

[87] William Hazlitt, "The Difference in Writing and Speaking," *Miscellaneous Works* (New York, 1869).

[88] *Lectures on Preaching*, p. 160.

[89] This practice is quite different from that of the Rev. Harry Emerson Fosdick. "I should be wretchedly unhappy not to have this whole matter clearly in mind and the initial stages of it stated by Tuesday noon at the latest. On Wednesday, Thursday, and Friday morning I work on the development of my strategy in achieving my goal that I have in mind with the congregation. Uniformly I am through with my manuscript on Friday noon. The next stage is one

most mature and then he would usher that one from the depths of the subconscious[90] to the fringe of the conscious. Then he would, moments later, in the pulpit permit the thoughts to step more boldly from the fringe of the conscious over the threshold of the conscious into being.[91]

C

Having considered the various fields from which Beecher gathered his ideas, and having treated the creative process that shaped these diverse ideas into new concepts, I shall now take up the nature of the proofs employed by Beecher. In the pulpit Beecher stamped his ideas with a religious significance. While nothing that was of interest to man was foreign to his preaching, and while he went on the principle that the pulpit

---

of the most important of all, for fearful that in working out my subject I may occasionally have forgotten my object, and may have got out of the center of focus the concrete personalities who will face me on Sunday, I sit down on Saturday morning and re-think the whole business as if the congregation were visibly before my eyes, often picking out individuals, and imaginatively trying my course of thought upon them, so as to be absolutely sure that I have not allowed any pride of discussion or lure of rhetoric to deflect me from my major purpose of doing something worth while with people. This process often means the elision of paragraphs that I liked very much when I first wrote them, and the rearrangement of order of thought in the interest of psychological persuasiveness. My sermon is always ready for the pulpit Saturday noon" ("Animated Conversation," *If I Had Only One Sermon to Prepare* [New York, 1932], p. 112).

[90] John Galsworthy, *The Creation of Character*, p. 5, suggests that the artist has this power to a greater degree than ordinary people. "The lecturer suspects that what we call our conscious or directive minds are normally only able to make a very limited and severely practical selective use of the treasures in our cellars, and that what we know as the creative gift in literature, or indeed in any art, is a more than normal power in certain people for dipping into the storehouse and fishing up the odds and ends of experience, together with a special aptitude for welding or grouping these odds and ends when they are fished up."

[91] Graham Wallas, *The Art of Thought* (New York, 1926), pp. 80–81, calls these four stages which I have just recapitulated, preparation, incubation, illumination, and verification.

should not ignore current affairs and politics, he believed that preaching should never descend to lecturing.

I claim that the pulpit has a right and a duty to discuss social questions—moral questions in politics, slavery, war, peace, and the intercourse of nations. It has a right to discuss commerce, industry, political economy; everything from the roof-tree to the foundation stone of the household, and everything that is of interest to the state. You have a duty to speak of all these things. There is not so broad a platform in the world as the Christian pulpit, nor an air so free as the heavenly air that overhangs it. You have a right and a duty to preach on all these things; but if you make your ministry to stand on them, it will be barren. It will be rather a lectureship than a Christian ministry. It will be secular and will become secularized. The real root and secret power, after all, in the pulpit, is the preaching of the invisible God to the people as an ever-present God.[92]

The lecturer desires to impart knowledge; the preacher to persuade men to a better life.

In order to persuade others to a nobler manhood, Beecher felt that it was obligatory that the preacher be a good man as well as an intelligent one. To persuade others a preacher must, in addition to intelligence and virtue, possess conviction and enthusiasm. In discussing what he termed the "moral beauty" of the preacher, Beecher is considering that instrument of persuasion which Aristotle termed ethical proof. Of this sort of proof, Aristotle said:

Ethical proof is wrought when the speech is so spoken as to make the speaker credible; for we trust good men more and sooner, as a rule, about everything, while, about things which do not admit of precision, but only of guess-work, we trust them absolutely. Now this trust, too, ought to be produced by means of the speech—not by a previous conviction that the speaker is this or that sort of man. It is not true, as some technical writers assume in their systems, that the moral worth of the speaker

[92] *Yale Lectures* (1st ser.), p. 110; the breadth of the pulpit is also mentioned on p. 80; it is also stressed in his sermon "Sphere of the Christian Ministry," R. G. Haweis, *Henry Ward Beecher in the Pulpit* (London, 1886), p. 99.

contributes nothing to his persuasiveness; nay, it might be said that almost the most authoritative of proofs is that supplied by character.[93]

The subjects of preaching do not admit of precision; they are largely speculative. The following passage from Beecher bears much the same thought as that of Aristotle.

While physical truth and abstract philosophy need not depend on the character of the teacher, yet all social and all moral truth depend largely upon the living exemplification of them. A man's calculations in astronomy have nothing to do with whether he is a curmudgeon or a gentleman; a man's deductions in geology, a man's teaching in botany have nothing to do with his personal character. The meanest man in the university may, after all, be one of the clearest men in the production of truth. All that class of truth that belongs to the senses and, as we may say, to the outside of man does not depend upon the character of the man that teaches it; but all that truth that is social that has relation to the affections and sympathies of mankind, and all that truth that is spiritual, that lifts a man up into the ideal, into a higher conception of right and duty, and the beauty of love and the service of God and the hope of immortality—all these truths do largely depend upon the man that teaches them.[94]

In his customary concrete manner, Beecher thus states that ethical proof is wrought in the minds of the listeners by the character of the speaker. The same truth is contained in his pithy remark, "Let no sneak try to be an orator."[95] The persuasive nature of the speaker's character has been a subject that has been discussed by rhetoricians down through the ages. Plato in the *Gorgias* mentions the importance of character in speaking. Quintilian[96] quotes with approval Cato's definition

[93] *The Rhetoric*, 1355a, Jebb's translation; Aristotle divided all proof into ethical, pathetic, and logical.

[94] J. B. Pond, "True Preaching," *A Summer in England with Henry Ward Beecher* (London, 1886), p. 135.

[95] *Lecture on Oratory* (Philadelphia, 1876).

[96] *Institute of Oratory* (tr. by J. S. Watson) (London, 1873), Book XII, chaps. i, iv.

of an orator, "a good man skilled in speaking." Hugh Blair, writing on pulpit oratory, said, "Now, if this be the proper idea of a sermon, a persuasive oration, one very material consequence follows that the preacher, himself, in order to be successful, must be a good man."[97] Many such quotations could be given, but, perhaps, that is unnecessary. It is undoubtedly more true of preaching than in other types of speaking that the character of the preacher acts as proof. It would be difficult to maintain, however, that no one can be persuasive who is not a good man. History records many orators whose characters were not above reproach. In single speeches, where the audience has no opportunity of knowing the character of the speaker, it is reputation that acts as an element of proof.

In addition to ethical proof, preaching lays emphasis upon pathetic proof, Beecher held. Rational, indeed, the preacher should always attempt to be; he should give the congregation clear issues on every subject, but his primary purpose is not that of the reasoner. Persuasion is his object.

Every man should preach two kinds of sermons; one for direct power on men's hearts and minds, and the other for their broadening in knowledge; but of this last class, less and less in our time, because the people have so many other sources of knowledge, and so many other training influences are going on in the community.[98]

Beecher felt that in an age when the press was so active in disseminating information, the pulpit should emphasize the appeals to the emotional life of his congregation. The sermon should give men and women an impulse toward a better life.

Beecher preached on the theory that the majority of people are reached through appeals to their emotions. He knew the truth of Cicero's remark, "Mankind make far more determina-

[97] *Lectures on Rhetoric and Belles Lettres* (Brooklyn, 1807), Lecture XXIX.

[98] *Yale Lectures* (1st ser.), p. 18; emphasis upon emotional proof is stressed on pages 16, 17, 24, 54, and 55.

tions through hatred, or love, or desire, or anger, or grief, or joy, or hope, or fear, or error, or some other affection of mind, than from regard to truth, or any settled maxim, or principle of right, or judicial form or adherence to laws."[99] And he also knew the weight of Hugh Blair's remark, apropos of preaching: "To be an accurate reasoner will be small praise, if he be not a persuasive speaker also."[100] It is not the business of the preacher to convince his congregation, for he deals with themes that are for the most part already believed. To question these accepted doctrines will raise up a "generation of chronic doubters." To persuade, not to convince, is the aim of preaching.

If you are going to preach, do not take things about which you are in doubt to lay before your people. Do not *prove* things too much. A man who goes into his pulpit every Sunday to prove things gives occasion for people to say, "Well, that is not half so certain as I thought it was." You will, by this course, raise up a generation of chronic doubters, and will keep them so by a little drilling in the nice refinement of doctrinal criticism. Do not employ arguments any more than is necessary and then only for the sake of answering objections and killing the enemies of the truth; but in so far as truth is concerned, preach it to the *consciousness* of men. If you have not spoiled your people, you have them on your side already. The Word of God and the laws of truth are all conformable to reason and to the course of things that now are; and, certainly, everything that is required in a Christian life—repentance for sin and turning from it, the taking hold of a higher manhood, the nobility, and disinterestedness of man—goes with God's Word and laws naturally. Assume your position, therefore; and if a man says to you, "How is it that you are so successful while using so little argument?" tell him that is the very reason of your success. Take things for granted, and men will not think to dispute them, but will admit them, and go on with you and become better men than if they had been treated to a logical process of argument, which aroused in them an argumentative spirit of doubt and opposition.[101]

[99] *De oratore* (tr. J. S. Watson [New York, 1860]), Book II, chap. xlii.

[100] "Lecture on Preaching," *Rhetoric and Belles Lettres*.

[101] *Yale Lectures* (1st series), pp. 124–125.

Beecher knew that preaching is forever getting away from appeals to the emotional life into intellectual disputes. Preaching is forever forgetting that its purpose is to ennoble mankind, to transform the dispositions of men, and is continually running amuck on intellectual subtleties. Recently, President George Cutten, of Colgate University, in a series of addresses given before the students of Colgate-Rochester Theological School said: "The weakness of the present-day theology is its lack of emotional appeal."[102] Its weakness in Beecher's time was the same and he set about to correct it.

The hard reasoner says, "No tears for me, don't color your preaching; I want it pure as the beams of light, and as transparent; and the calmer and more inexorably logical its propositions, and the more mathematical its proof, the better I like it." But there are in any community probably six to one who will watch for the emotional and impassioned part of the sermon saying, "That is the preaching I want; I can understand what I feel." They are fed by their hearts. They have as much right to be fed by their hearts as others have to be fed by their reason.[103]

The ones who are fed by their reason are not to be neglected but the emphasis in preaching should be on pathetic proof since the majority of people are reached in that way, and since the dissemination of knowledge by means of the press relieves the pulpit of that responsibility. Although believing that the emphasis should be on pathetic proof, Beecher also said: "There ought to be in every sermon something that shall task your audience somewhat as it tasked you; otherwise you will not compass some of the noblest themes that lie in the sphere of your duty."[104]

The four fundamental themes of Beecher's preaching were concerned with appeals to the hearts of men primarily. They were (1) a suffering God, (2) Jesus, as a revelation of the love of

[102] *The Baptist* (December 20, 1930), p. 1585.

[103] *Yale Lectures* (1st ser.), p. 54.   [104] *Ibid.*, p. 157.

God, (3) the sanctity of the individual, and (4) the certainty of the soul's immortality. In one word, the subject matter of Beecher's sermons was love—love of God and love of man.

Typical sermon titles bear out the emphasis upon his appeal to the emotions; some of these are: "Heart-House," "Saved by Hope," "The Primacy of Love," "Summer in the Soul," "God's Grace," "Christian Sympathy," "Soul-Power," "Soul-Relationship," "Christian Joyfulness," "The Immortality of Good Work." He concluded, characteristically enough, his first series of *Yale Lectures on Preaching*, with an address on "Love, The Central Element of the Ministry."

In writing on Beecher, Vernon L. Parrington[105] calls him the high priest of emotionalism. This epithet would have delighted Beecher. Testimony as to the emotional warmth of Beecher's speaking is seen in the following quotation from one of the letters of Charles Eliot Norton: "Last night we went to hear Beecher. He spoke admirably, and it was a great pleasure to hear him. It was not great oratory, but it was a fine, large, broad, sensible, human, sympathetic performance. Tomorrow we have a dinner of our Dozen Club for him."[106] The note struck here, i.e., *human* and *sympathetic*, is the prevailing note of Beecher's speaking. Everett, Phillips, and Sumner excelled Beecher in the powers of analysis and lucid exposition, but Beecher was superior in mastering the emotions and exciting the enthusiasm of an audience.

One of the instruments used in arousing the audience was humor.[107] Beecher could sweep the audience with laughter as

[105] *The Beginnings of Critical Realism* (New York, 1930), p. 95.

[106] Sarah Norton, *Letters of Charles Eliot Norton* (New York, 1913), I, 266.

[107] The following volume is listed in the *Auction Sale Catalogue*: "Wit and Humor of the Age," by Mark Twain, Josh Billings, Robert J. Burdette, Alex Sweet, Eli Perkins, with the "Philosophy of Wit and Humor," by Melville D. Landon (Chicago, 1883).

easily as he could reduce them to tears. In his use of humor in the pulpit he was unconventional and was often criticized for its use. When asked if it was proper to make an audience laugh in church by means of an illustration, he replied:

Never turn aside from a laugh any more than you would from a cry. Go ahead on your Master's business, and do it well. And remember this, that every faculty in you was placed there by the dear Lord God for his service. Never *try* to raise a laugh for a laugh's sake, or to make men merry as a piece of sensationalism, when you are preaching on solemn things. That is allowable at a picnic, but not in a pulpit where you are preaching to men in regard to God and their own destiny. But if mirth comes up naturally, do not stifle it; strike that chord, and particularly if you want to make an audience cry. If I can make them laugh, I do not thank anybody for the next move; I will make them cry.[108]

This is the extent of Beecher's remarks on humor. He mentions his use of humor and the fact that he has often been criticized for employing humor in the pulpit in his "Address to Students," but he does not enlarge upon the above statement. Humor in the pulpit has always been unconventional and frowned upon. Francis Bacon[109] (1597) warned against its use in speaking on religious themes. Even today humor in the pulpit is to be used sparingly, if at all.[110] Outside the pulpit, however, the legitimacy and power of humor as a factor in persuasion has long been recognized. Ancient rhetoricians[111] have passages devoted to its use.

[108] *Yale Lectures* (1st ser.), p. 178.

[109] *Of Discourse.*

[110] H. W. Taft, *Conversation and Public Speaking* (New York, 1929), p. 182. "In the pulpit a preacher may illustrate a precept or enforce an argument by a homely illustration that may evoke a smile, but there is always danger in offending the sensibilities of the too serious-minded and those who believe that there should be no relaxation of the solemnity of time-honored conventions of the Divine service."

[111] Aristotle *The Rhetoric* iii. 18. 7. 1419b; Cicero *De oratore* ii. 54; Quintilian *Institutes of Oratory* vi. 31.

Beecher never made humor an end in the pulpit; it was a means of actuating men. David Macrae testifies that Beecher used humor as an instrument to persuade men to a better life.

People quote Beecher's funny sayings as they used to quote Spurgeon's, but these are mere bubbles on the surface of the rushing stream. You may have laughed with the others at some odd illustration, but you leave the church a better man than when you entered it. You have got an impulse in the right direction. You go away with higher thoughts and purposes; this, after all, is the test of a good sermon. Of the two extremes it is better to laugh and get good, than to sleep and get none.[112]

With what effectiveness humor was employed in winning the audiences in England in 1863 can be judged by the frequent interpolations of the word "laughter" in the unedited copy of the speeches. Passages of humor from Beecher's works have found their way into a book of American Humor,[113] and a 213-page book[114] of humorous selections from his works has been compiled.

While Beecher aimed to make his preaching emotional in character, avoiding argument as much as possible, his speeches on secular occasions often mingled logical with pathetic proof. It will be recalled in a previous quotation Beecher said apropos of the employment of logical appeals, "Do not employ arguments any more than is necessary and then only for the sake of answering objections and killing the enemies of the truth." There were many occasions during his life when he felt that there was necessity for the use of refutation and the upholding of the truth. The "Liverpool Address" grew out of a situation demanding argument as well as persuasion. At the beginning of his speech, Beecher said, "If I cannot carry you with me by

[112] David Macrae, *The Treasury of Modern Biography* (London, 1878), pp. 445–50.

[113] *American Humor*, Putnam & Sons, 1907.

[114] Eleanor Kirk, *Henry Ward Beecher as a Humorist* (New York, 1887), pp. 213.

facts and sound arguments, I do not wish you to go with me at all." Beecher used not only facts and sound arguments but he used appeals to the emotions of his audience. The Englishman's love of fair play, his love for his native land, his sympathy for the down-trodden are joined with logical appeals. The "Liverpool Address" is, no doubt, the best example, in modern oratory, of the argumentative and pathetic acting in concert. Of this type of oratory, addressed to the passions and the intellect, George Campbell said:

Finally, as that kind, the most complex of all, which is calculated to influence the will, and persuade to a certain conduct, is in reality an artful mixture of that which proposes to convince the judgment, and that which interests the passions, its distinguishing excellency results from these two, the argumentative and the pathetic incorporated together. These acting with united force, and, if I may so express myself, in concert, constitute that passionate eviction, that vehemence of contention, which is admirably fitted for persuasion, and hath always been regarded as the supreme qualification in an orator. It is this which bears down every obstacle, and procures the speaker an irresistible power over the thoughts, and purposes of his audience. It is this which hath been so justly celebrated as giving one man an ascendent over others, superior even to what despotism itself can bestow; since by the latter the more ignoble part only, the body and its members are enslaved; whereas from the dominion of the former, nothing is exempted, neither judgment nor affection, not even the inmost recesses, the most latent movements of the soul. What opposition is he not prepared to conquer, on whose arms reason hath conferred solidity and weight, and passion such a sharpness as enables them, in defiance of every obstruction, to open a speedy passage to the heart?[115]

In the "Liverpool Address" Beecher exhibited the supreme qualification of the orator thus described by Campbell. To illustrate Beecher's use of logical proof I shall confine myself to showing his use of facts, reasoning, opinions, and examples.

The following paragraph shows his use of statistics:

[115] George Campbell, *The Philosophy of Rhetoric* (7th ed. [London, 1823]), Book I, chap. i, p. 16.

Now, for instance, just look at this, the difference between free labor and slave labor to produce cultivated land. The State of Virginia has 15,000 more square miles of land than the State of New York; but Virginia has only 15,000 square miles improved, while New York has 20,000 square miles improved. Of the unimproved land Virginia has about 23,000 square miles, and New York only about 10,000 square miles. These facts speak volumes as to the capacity of the territory to bear population. The smaller is the quantity of soil uncultivated, the greater is the density of the population—[*hear, hear*];—and upon that their value depends. Let us take the states of Maryland and Massachusetts. Maryland has 2,000 more square miles of land than Massachusetts; but Maryland has about 4,000 square miles of land improved, Massachusetts has 3,200 square miles. Maryland has 2,800 unimproved square miles of land, while Massachusetts has but 1,800 square miles unimproved. But these two are little states—let us take greater States: Pennsylvania and Georgia, etc.

There is an entire page of such statistics in the "Liverpool Address" showing the difference between the capacity of free labor and slave labor to produce cultivated land.

As an instance of his reasoning with an audience, let us consider Beecher's use of the enthymeme, which Aristotle said was one of the two forms of proof. Beecher's statement, "Poor and ignorant people buy little and that of the poorest kind. The richest and the intelligent having the more means to buy, buy the most and buy the best," could easily be reduced to a syllogism. Again, "That nation is the best customer that is freest," is an abridged syllogism. And, once more, "It is my old acquaintance; I understand it perfectly and I have always held it to be an unfailing truth that where a man had a cause that would bear examination he was perfectly willing to have it spoken about," lets the audience supply one of the premises of the implied syllogism. These are but a few of the enthymemes occurring in the "Liverpool Address."

Beecher does not make great use of the opinions of others in his speaking. In the "Liverpool Address" there are but three instances when he supports his position with the testimony of others. One is from the editor of the *Virginia Times*, another from Lord Russell, and the third is from President Lincoln.

Beecher makes most use of the example as a form of proof. Beecher regarded the example, or the illustration, as the best weapon in the hands of one who speaks to large assemblies of the common people. The illustration was essential to him in bringing emotional and intellectual appeals to bear upon the hearts and minds of his audience. The importance of the illustration in his rhetorical theory is evident in that he devoted one entire lecture of the *Yale Lectures on Preaching* to this means of persuasion; usually in textbooks on public speaking, the illustration is given a brief paragraph. His handling of the illustration was assiduously cultivated.

In regard to illustration, you will find many persons who are instinctively given to it. Many of you will find it natural to you. But do not be discouraged, even when it is natural, if you do not at once succeed. Why should you succeed before you learn the rudiments of your art? Practice by yourselves to imaginary audiences; make illustrations and use them; train yourselves to it. If once or twice on every Sabbath day you can make a fitting illustration and see that you have gained ground by it, take courage, and you will improve day by day and year by year. I can say for your encouragement, that while illustrations are as natural to me as breathing, I use fifty now to one in the early years of my ministry. For the first six or eight years, perhaps, they were comparatively few and far apart. But I developed myself in that respect; and that, too, by study and practice, by hard thought, and by a great many trials, both with the pen, and extemporaneously by myself, when I was walking here and there. Whatever I have gained in that direction is largely the result of education.[116]

Although Beecher's most complete treatment of the illustration appears in the *Yale Lectures on Preaching*, first series, he often referred[117] to its importance in the course of his other

[116] *Yale Lectures* (1st ser.), p. 175.

[117] Beecher refers to the importance of the illustration in his *Life of Christ* (New York: J. B. Ford & Co. [1871]), I, 401; also in *Lecture Room Talks* (New York, 1872), p. 203; *Yale Lectures* (2d ser.), pp. 92, 94, 102, 156.

works. The eleven uses of the illustration which I find mentioned by him are: (1) narration; (2) explanation; (3) assist
proof; (4) add ornament; (5) arouse attention; (6) assist memory; (7) introduce humor; (8) stimulate the imagination; (9)
provide for various hearers; (10) bridge difficult places; (11)
educate the people to use illustrations, and thus be led "into
the truth." I shall take up these aspects in turn for detailed
consideration. Before doing this, however, it might be well to
understand what Beecher meant by the illustration.

> Experience has taught that not only are persons pleased by being in
> structed through illustration, but they are more readily instructed thus,
> because, substantially, the mode in which we learn a new thing is by its
> being likened to something which we already know. They are a kind of
> covert analogy, or likening one thing to another, so that obscure things
> become plain, being represented pictorially or otherwise by things that
> are not obscure and that we are familiar with.[118]

The illustration depends upon the principle of reference to
experience, or of likening the unknown to the known.

1. The illustration may introduce the narrative quality. It
is not strange that Beecher should treat this aspect of the illustration, for the Bible, which he studied most sedulously, is
written largely in the narrative form. Christ employed more
than thirty parables in his teachings. Cicero, thus, calls attention to the pleasure that is furnished by the narrative element,
"A narrative referring to various characters, and intersected by
dialogue, affords much gratification."[119] Indeed, we never outgrow our interest in the story, which begins in childhood, as
Beecher says:

> Then, next, it seems to me we should attempt to teach our children as
> much as possible, as the Scripture teaches us, by narrative. You never
> had to persuade a child to listen to a parable. You never had to persuade
> a child to listen while you read a thrilling history. The Bible is written
> largely in the narrative style.[120]

[118] *Yale Lectures* (1st ser.), p. 155.   [119] *De oratore* ii. 180.
[120] *Lecture Room Talks* (New York, 1872), p. 203.

The *Yale Lectures on Preaching* owe much of their charm to the illustrations drawn from Beecher's own experience. Many of these illustrations are animated with characters and dialogue. The narrative quality is present.

2. The illustration may be used to make a statement clear. The word *illustrate* means literally to throw light or luster upon anything. The illustration should never be regarded as an end in itself; it lights up some argument, some weighty truth, some principle of life. As Beecher said, "Now an illustration is a window in an argument, and lets in light."[121] And in another connection, he declared: "The purpose that we have in view in employing an illustration is to help the people to understand more easily the things that we are teaching them." This use of the illustration, as would be expected, is the most commonly mentioned in textbooks on rhetoric.

3. Illustrations may assist proof. Aristotle[122] declared that there are only two forms of proof, examples and enthymemes. Inductive reasoning depends upon the use of numerous examples. The truth of the general principle in deductive reasoning is often made clear by the use of examples. The illustration is in and of itself a ground of probability; in modern science many important discoveries have been suggested by analogy. Beecher knew that frequently a striking analogy will do more to convince the wavering, to establish the weak in faith, than a whole volume of philosophic argument. A large audience needs truth put in concrete terms. "An argument," Beecher stated, "may as well go forward by illustration as by abstract

[121] *Yale Lectures* (1st ser.), p. 155.

[122] Aristotle *The Rhetoric* 1356*b*, states: "All men effect their proofs by demonstration either with examples or with enthymemes, there is no third way." Cicero *De oratore* iii. 53: "The illustration has wonderful influence in giving a representation of any affair, both to illustrate what is represented, and to amplify it, so that the point we amplify may appear to the audience to be really as great as the powers of our language represent it."

statement; sometimes it will go better."[123] As a means of persuasion the study of the art of illustration is as important as the study of logic.

4. Illustrations may ornament a discourse. William Taylor tells of the workman who stated that we must never "construct ornament, but only ornament construction."[124] Surely, this principle applies to the employment of illustrations. Illustrations may ornament an address but they must not have that as their chief end. If an illustration is admired for its felicity alone it is worse than useless, for it detracts from the idea that is being presented. But if an illustration happens to give splendor to the discourse there is no objection. "An illustration," Beecher declared, "is never to be a mere ornament, although being an ornament is no objection to it."[125] It is easy to see how illustrations drawn from wide areas of human experience would give a certain brilliancy to an address. "Comparisons," as Demetrius said, "are full of charm."[126]

5. Impressions produced by striking illustrations are easily remembered. An intricate argument may soon be forgotten but if fastened to an illustration it stands a very good chance of being remembered. Like a nail, the illustration fastens the argument to the mind.

Then they (illustrations) are a very great help in carrying away and remembering the things your audience have heard from you; because it is true from childhood up that we remember pictures and parables and fables and stories. Now if in your discourses when taking a comprehensive view of truth, you illustrate each step by an appropriate picture, you will

[123] *Yale Lectures* (1st ser.), p. 165.

[124] William Taylor, *The Ministry of the Word* (New York, 1876), p. 185.

[125] *Yale Lectures* (1st ser.), p. 160.

[126] Demetrius *On Style* 160; Cicero mentions this use of the illustration in *De Oratore* iii. 38; Quintilian said, "Similitudes are sometimes sought merely for the embellishment of the speech" (*Institutes of Oratory* v. 1); Phillips Brooks, *Lectures on Preaching*, p. 175, states that splendor along with clearness is a legitimate use of the illustration.

find that the plain people of your congregation will go away, remembering every one of your illustrations. If they are asked, 'Well, what was the illustration for?' they will stop and consider; 'What was he saying then?' They will fish for it, and will generally get the substance of it. 'O, it was this; he was proving so and so, and then he illustrated it by this.' They will remember the picture; and, if they are questioned, the picture will bring back the truth to them and after that they will remember both together. Whereas all except the few logically trained minds would very soon have forgotten what you had discoursed upon, if you had not thus suitably seasoned it. Your illustrations will be the salt that will preserve your teachings, and men will remember them.[127]

Beecher believed that the discourse was only half finished when it was delivered. He wanted the audience to think over what he had said. Here is the true artist in Beecher asserting itself. If conduct was to be changed, the audience had to take to heart and remember what he said.

One should remember that a lecture is but just begun when a lecturer has finished its delivery. The audience have laughed and clapped, glowed or wept, admired or yawned, as the case may be, and social sympathy has carried them along pretty much together. Now they disperse. They begin to talk on their way home. The father and the mother draw the children out, to know how much they heard, and what the impression was produced on them, they discuss it, and the family for several days is a debating society. Young men in an office, clerks in a store, mechanics in the shop, boys in the academy, all overhaul the lecture, and for a week it becomes a theme of reflection, discussion, and active criticism. In this way one lecture controls another.[128]

[127] *Yale Lectures* (1st ser.), p. 159. This idea of the illustration appears first in the history of rhetorical illustration, as far as I am able to discover, in a book called *The Power of Illustration, An Element of Success in Preaching and Teaching* (New York, 1850). It occurs next in *The Parables* (New York, 1870), by Thomas Guthrie; after Beecher's *Yale Lectures*, it has frequently been cited as one of the uses of the illustration. There is no difference between Beecher's explanation of this use and that of the others.

[128] Henry Ward Beecher, *Eyes and Ears* (New York, 1855), p. 103, essay on "The Lecture System." Coleridge (*Literary Remains*, II, 4), stated, "The day of the lecture I devote to the consideration of how to leave a sting behind, that is, a desire to study the subject anew, under the light of a new principle."

6. Another of the uses enumerated by Beecher is that humor may be introduced into the speech by means of an illustration. When asked if there was an objection to using an illustration that produced laughter, he replied, "Never turn aside from a laugh any more than you would from a cry."[129] I have shown in the discussion of pathetic proof that Beecher depended much upon humor as an instrument of persuasion. The illustration offered a convenient vehicle for its introduction into a discourse. In the following quotation from the "Liverpool Address," the humor of the illustration was not lost upon the audience.

Nothing could be more generous, when a weak party stands for its own legitimate rights against imperious pride and power, than to sympathize with the weak. But whoever yet sympathized with a weak thief, because three constables had got hold of him? [Hear, hear.] And yet the one thief in three policemen's hands is the weaker party; I suppose *you* would sympathize with him! [Hear, hear, laughter, and applause.]

Much of Beecher's humor in the use of illustrations came from unexpected comparisons. He showed relations where the audience had not discerned any.

7. Again, illustrations may stimulate the imagination and thus aid the audience to participate in the address. Beecher desired the audience to think along with him. He found that the illustration because it was concrete, because it used narrative, "intersected with character and dialogue," aroused the imagination of his congregation. From its own subconscious mind the audience drew up parallel images.

The effect of illustrations upon ideality is very great. Illustrations bring into play the imaginative faculty, which is only another name for

[129] *Yale Lectures* (1st ser.), p. 178; the first mention of the fact that humor may be introduced into a speech by means of the illustration occurs in Cicero's *De Oratore* ii. 66. Its use is recognized in Professor Mosher's study. I do not find it again until Beecher's treatment. It appears again in H. W. Taft's *Conversation and Public Speaking*, p. 182.

ideality. In no other way can you stir up that side of the mind to grasp your statements and arguments so easily, and prepare it to remember them. You cannot help your audience in any other way so well as by keeping alive in them the sense of imagination, and making the truth palpable to them, because it is appealing to the taste, to the sense of the beautiful in imagery as well as to the sense of the truth.[130]

8. Illustrations, also, Beecher declared educate the people to think for themselves. He wanted to make "the truth palpable to them"; he wanted the audience to think for itself.

I notice that in a prayer-meeting which has grown up under a minister who illustrates, all the members of the church illustrate too. They all begin to see visions, and to catch likenesses and resemblances. This becomes a habit, and it is to them a pathfinder or a starfinder, as it were. It leads men to look at truth, not only in one aspect, but in all its bearings, and to make analogies and illustrations for themselves, and thus brings them into the truth. By this means you bring up your congregation to understand the truth more easily than you would by any other method.[131]

This statement reminds one of that sentence from De Quincey: "Now to apprehend and detect more relations, or to pursue them steadily, is a process absolutely impossible without the intervention of physical analogies."[132] There can be no advance in knowledge except as the audience appropriates the truth to themselves. The heart of all communicative processes[133] is to make the audience realize the truth through their

[130] *Yale Lectures* (1st ser.), pp. 159–60; it is in Professor Mosher's study that I first find this use of the illustration mentioned. Next, I find it in Guthrie's book, *The Parables*. A. E. Phillips (*Effective Speaking* [Chicago, 1908], p. 107), and C. R. Brown (*The Art of Preaching* [New York, 1924], p. 129), notice this use of the illustration.

[131] *Yale Lectures*, pp. 159–60.

[132] *Essays on Style, Rhetoric and Language*, ed. F. N. Scott (Boston, 1893), p. 173.

[133] Hugh Blair mentioned this use of the illustration. He said: "Illustrations prompt us to remark and observe and thereby make us advance in useful knowledge" (*Lectures on Rhetoric and Belles Lettres*, I, 241 ff.). Cardinal John Henry Newman has stated that it is the purpose of education to make a man conscious

own experience.[134] If the speaker can start cerebration along the lines he chooses, he is on the road to success. The use of illustrations, comparison, is a way of thinking; the audience begins with its own experience and by contrast and comparison enters new realms of thought. This is another instance of Beecher's desire to stir up thought in the audience.

9. Illustrations may rest the audience by appealing to different "parts of the mind." Beecher's reading of phrenology is perhaps responsible for his phraseology, and although we may be disposed to dislike his terminology, his meaning is clear.

It is a great art to know how to preach as long as you want to, or have to, and yet not tire your audience, especially where you have been preaching many years in the same place. For my own part I do not think that a very long sermon is adapted to edification; but a man ought to be able to preach an hour, and to hold his audience, too. He cannot do it, however, if his sermon is a monotone either in voice or thought. He cannot do it unless it is interesting. He cannot possibly hold his people unwearied, when they have been accustomed to his voice, his manner, and his thoughts, unless he moves through a very considerable scale, up and down, resting them; in other words, changing the faculties that he is addressing. For instance, you at one time, by statements of fact, engage the perspective reason. You soon pass, by natural transition, to the relations that exist between facts and statements, and you are then addressing another audience, namely, the reflective faculties of your people. And when you have concluded an argument upon that, and have flashed an illustration that touches and wakes up their fancy and imagination you are bringing in still another audience—namely the ideal or imaginative

of his own opinions and judgments. He said, "It is the education which gives a man a clear, conscious view of his own opinions and judgments, a truth in developing them, and eloquence in expressing them, and a force in urging them" (*The Aim of a University Education*).

[134] John Keats emphasizes that we must experience the truth for ourselves. "In regard to his genius alone, we find what he (Wordsworth) says true as far as we have experienced, and we can judge no further but by larger experience . . . . for axioms in philosophy are not axioms until they are proved upon our pulses" (Letter to Reynolds, May, 1818).

one. And, now, if out of these you express a sweet wine that goes to the emotions and arouses their feelings so that one and another in the congregation wipes his eyes, and the proud man, that does not want to cry, blows his nose—what have you done? You have relieved the weariness of your congregation by enabling them to listen with different parts of their minds to what you have been saying.[135]

This economy of the attention of the audience was no doubt suggested to Beecher by Herbert Spencer's essay on "The Philosophy of Style," which, I have shown, Beecher studied. Spencer, however, does not discuss this use of the illustration, nor does any other rhetorician before Beecher. A careful student of rhetoric, John A. Broadus, gives Beecher credit for suggesting this use of the illustration to him in his discussion of the illustration in his revised edition of *The Preparation and Delivery of Sermons* (1898). Broadus' book first appeared in 1870. In this edition, there is no mention of the power of illustrations to rest the audience. In his revised edition he includes this use and, as the following quotation indicates, suggested that Beecher was the source of the idea.

They [illustrations] are in this respect even more serviceable in the progress of the discourse particularly if the attention has been somewhat strained by argument or description, and begins to flag. They thus, as Beecher says, afford variety and rest to the mind; and this is important.[136]

10. Another use of the illustration is that it provides for various hearers.

The relation of illustrations to a mixed audience is another point which deserves careful consideration. . . . . You are bound to see *that everybody gets something every time.* There ought not to be a five-year-old child that shall go home without something that pleases and instructs him. . . . . There always ought to be, and there is no way in which you can prepare a sermon for the delectation of the plain people, and the uncultured, and little children, better than by making it attractive and instructive with

[135] *Yale Lectures* (1st ser.), p. 160.

[136] J. A. Broadus, *The Preparation and Delivery of Sermons* (revised ed.) (New York, 1898), p. 227.

illustrations. It is always the best method with a mixed audience. You
are to preach so that every man shall have his portion in due season, and
that portion ought to be in every sermon, more or less. You will scarcely
be able to do it in any other way than by illustration. If God has not given
you the gift by original endowment, strive to attain it by cultivation.[137]

This use of the illustration, when brought to our attention,
seems perfectly obvious. The preacher's audience, more so
than any other, is heterogeneous. Adults might appreciate the
felicity of the illustration while children might enjoy the story
element. Because the illustration is capable of ornament, of
appeals to the imagination, of assisting proof, of stimulating
thought, it is invaluable for reaching all levels of society. It
was undoubtedly Beecher's skill in using the illustration that
prompted Anna de Bremont to remark, "He had the charm of
bringing his subject within the scope of the most limited understanding."[138] Professor W. N. Brigance includes this use of the
illustration in his discussion of this instrument of persuasion
and credits Beecher as the source.

11. The last use of the illustration given by Beecher suggests that he thought of rhetoric as the art of appearance.
Illustrations often permit the speaker to say indirectly what he
does not dare, or care, to say directly.

Illustrations are invisible tactics. A minister hovers between "ought
to do" and "how to do." He knows there is a subject that ought to be
preached about; and yet, if he should deliberately preach on that topic,
everybody would turn around and look at Mr. A., who is the very embodiment of that special vice or fault or excellence. There are many very
important themes which a minister may not desire to preach upon, for
various reasons, especially if he wish to remain in the parish. But there
are times when you can attain your object by an illustration pointed at
that topic, without indicating whom you are hitting, but continuing your
sermon as though you were utterly unconscious of the effect of your blow.

[137] *Yale Lectures* (1st ser.), p. 162.

[138] Anna de Bremont, "Henry Ward Beecher as an Actor," *The Theatre*,
XVIII (May 1, 1887), 246.

When I was settled at Indianapolis, nobody was allowed to say a word on the subject of slavery. They were all red-hot out there then; and one of the Elders said, "If an abolitionist comes here, I will head a mob and put him down." I was a young preacher. I had some pluck; and I felt, and it grew upon me, that that was a subject that ought to be preached upon; but I knew that just as sure as I preached an abolition sermon they would blow me sky high, and my usefulness in that parish would be gone. Yet, I was determined that they should hear it, first or last. The question was, "How shall I do it?" I recollect one of the earliest efforts I made in that direction was in a sermon on some general topic. It was necessary to illustrate a point, and I did it by picturing a father ransoming his son from captivity among the Algerines, and glorying in his love of liberty and his fight against bondage. They all thought I was going to apply it to slavery, but I did not. I applied it to my subject, and it passed off; and they all drew a long breath; it was not long before I had another illustration from that quarter. And so, before I had been there a year, I had gone over all the sore spots in slavery, in illustrating the subjects of Christian experience and doctrine. It broke the ice. You may say that was not the most honorable way and that it was a weakness. It may have been so; but I conquered them by that very weakness.[139]

This employment of the illustration while, perhaps, not generally useful would be particularly helpful to the preacher who finds that speaking bluntly on existing conditions is forbidden by discretion. An illustration in which the essentials remain the same but which disguises the details might accomplish the desired results without embarrassment.

The one outstanding characteristic of Beecher's sermons is their wealth of illustrations. No other instrument of persuasion did he cultivate so painstakingly. In 1904 there was published a 675-page volume[140] of illustrations selected from his published works. The book contains 2,585 illustrations. In addition to this book, there are such compilations as *Life*

---

[139] *Yale Lectures* (1st ser.), pp. 166, 167.

[140] *A Treasury of Illustrations*, selected from the works of H. W. Beecher, Introduction by Newell Dwight Hillis (New York: Revell, 1904).

Thoughts[141] (1858), *The Crown of Life* (1890), *Memorial to Beecher* (1887), *Metaphors and Similes* (1895), which are filled largely with illustrations from his works. Beecher's skill in the use of illustrations caused John A. Broadus[142] to mention him along with such other great preachers as St. Chrysostom, Jeremy Taylor, Christmas Evans, Chalmers, and Spurgeon. At his death in 1887, the *New York Tribune* said: "Thousands have marvelled at the variety and aptness of his illustrations without reflecting how vast must have been the stores of information upon which he drew."[143]

In order to show the relation of Beecher's treatment of the illustration to the past and present considerations of this instrument of persuasion, I have given below a table which attempts to record the uses of the illustration as they have been cited by important rhetoricians through the centuries. It will be noticed that the list of uses enumerated by Beecher is longer than the list of any one other rhetorician. Beecher gives eleven uses. It will be noticed, too, that after Beecher the treatment by rhetoricians is more detailed. And, finally, it will be noticed that Beecher states three uses of the illustration that are not set forth before his time; in other words, they appear as original deductions by him of the uses of the illustration. These are (1) the illustration provides for various hearers; (2) the illustration rests the audience by appealing to "different parts of the mind"; and (3) the illustration assists the speaker in stating his point indirectly. These three are given last under Beecher.

[141] W. M. Taylor, *The Ministry of the Word* (New York, 1876). One of the series of *Yale Lectures on Preaching* states that this book taught him the value of illustrative preaching.

[142] *The Preparation and Delivery of Sermons* (revised ed., New York, 1898), p. 216.

[143] *New York Tribune*, March 8, 1887.

Aristotle	*Cicero*	*Demetrius*	*Quintilian*
proof	humor	ornament	proof
	proof	force	ornament
	narrative		

J. A. Mosher, Ph.D. thesis
proof
imagination
clearness
attention
humor
to "farce" a sermon

Wilson (1553)
persuasion

Kames (1763)	*Campbell* (1773)	*Blair* (1775)
instinct	proof	ornament
force		clearness
vividness		force
impressiveness		instruct
		interest
		educates hearers to appreciate truth

Whately (1829)	*Newman, S. B* (1834)	*Dowling* (1850)
clearness	amplify	attention
proof	proof	variety of presentation
	ornament	memory
	clearness	explain
		interest
Vinet (1853)	*Broadus* (1870)	*Guthrie* (1870)
proof	explain	instruct
	proof	entertain
	ornament	attention
	impress	imagination
		memory

NINETEENTH CENTURY RHETORICIANS—*Continued*

Beecher (1872)
explanation
narration
proof
ornament
memory
humor
imagination
educates hearers to
  appreciate truth
rests attention
provides for various
  hearers
visible tactics

Taylor (1875)
clearness
proof
attention
memory
humor

Brooks (1876)
clearness
splendor

Phelps (1883)
explain
prove
impress

Fisk (1893)
clearness
vividness
memory
attractiveness

Spurgeon (1894)
attention
proof
memory
vividness
explain

Pattison (1896)
imagination
clearness

Broadus (1896)
explain
proof
ornament
impress
rests the audience (borrowed from Beecher)
assists the memory

TWENTIETH-CENTURY RHETORICIANS

Baldwin (1903)
clearness
attention

Hoyt (1905)
clearness
force
splendor
proof

Genung (1900)
proof

Shurter (1909)	*Phillips* (1908)	*Winans* (1916)
clearness	clearness	interest
proof	impressiveness	memory
memory	imagination	
	permanent popularity	
	belief	

C. R. Brown (1922)	*Mosher* (1924)	*O'Neill and Weaver* (1926)
clearness	forcefulness	vividness
memory		proof
imagination		
educates hearers to		
appreciate truth		

Brigance (1927)	*Williamson* (1930)	*Sandford and Yeager* (1930)
proof	proof	arouse interest
memory	clearness	proof
provides for various		clearness
hearers (borrowed		memory
from Beecher)		

It is perfectly fitting that I should close the discussion of
Beecher's rhetorical invention with a treatment of the illustration. All of his resourcefulness seemed to find expression in this
instrument of persuasion. His first-hand knowledge of mankind took the form of illustrations; his observations of nature's
laws were correlated with spiritual laws by means of the illustration; his omnivorous reading evinces itself in his discourses
through the employment of the illustration; his love of the
beautiful led people to a sense of God through the use of the
illustration. The illustration was suitable to a mingling of
pathetic and logical proof.

In the next section on arrangement it will become plain that
the illustration was adaptable to his theory of planning for
extempore speaking.

ARRANGEMENT

A. Importance of aim and plan
B. Audience and the plan
   1. Plan arising from needs of audience
   2. Preconceived plans not inviolable
   3. Unity of effect necessary
C. Modes of attack
   1. Suggestive preaching
   2. Line of fact and series of parables
   3. Ability to use logical plans
D. Analysis of practice
   1. "Address to Students"
   2. Prodigal Son sermon
   3. Spurgeon comparison

A

Demosthenes opens his *Oration on the Crown* by begging the court not to allow the petition of Aeschines to force him to follow the same arrangement of his material in answering the charges brought against him as Aeschines had employed in bringing those charges forward. Persuasion, Demosthenes realized, is as dependent upon the order of the arguments as upon the arguments themselves. No one was more cognizant of this rhetorical axiom than Beecher. He said: "No man ought to go into the pulpit with the direct kind of sermon without having a definite reason why he selected one subject rather than another, and why he put it in one form rather than another."[1]

[1] The necessity of taking aim in speaking is mentioned by Beecher on the following pages of the *Yale Lectures* (1st ser.), pp. 3, 4, 6, 7, 10, 19, 21, 29, 31, 38, 40, 41, 46, 48, 51, 60, 68, 78, 84, 97, 106, 121, 165, 214, 228; (2d ser.), p. 282; (3d ser.), p. 63; this emphasis occurs many times in his "Address to Students," "True Preaching," and "Successful Preaching."

B

The fact that the judge knew one side of the case made it imperative that the facts on Demosthenes' side be presented in another manner from that of his accuser. The point is, as has often been noted by rhetoricians,[2] the audience plays a part in determining the order of the ideas to be presented. This was the lesson Beecher learned from the sermons of Jonathan Edwards. He said: "I went eagerly through Edwards to see how he took aim." Beecher learned that the aim arose from meeting the needs of his congregation; it was the same principle that he learned from studying the preaching of the Apostles. Beecher described his own practice when he made the following observation concerning the preaching of St. Paul.

Romans derives its structure full as much from what the Jews were as from what Paul was. It was an argument of persuasion aimed at the peculiarities of his countrymen. Abstract thought in which order follows logical association was not his method. Like a surgeon, he watched the face and pulse of the patient at every motion of the knife.[3]

Just as St. Paul suited his aim and plan to the needs of his countrymen, Beecher shaped his sermon aim and plan to meet the needs of the people who crowded[4] to hear him. The adjustment

[2] Apropos of this principle Whately said (*Elements of Rhetoric*, Part I, chap. iii, sec. 5); "A proposition that is *well-known* (whether easy to be established or not) and which contains nothing particularly offensive, should in general be stated at once, and the Proofs subjoined; but one not familiar to the hearers, especially if it be likely to be unacceptable, should not be stated at the outset. It is usually better in that case to state the arguments first, or at least some of them, and then introduce the Conclusion: thus assuming in some degree the character of an investigator."

[3] Lyman Abbott, *Henry Ward Beecher* (New York, 1904), p. 423. Outline for sermon on "Paul's Theology."

[4] Beecher understood that it was necessary to crowd the congregation together if he was to render them suggestible. His church seated, when completely filled, 3,000 people. The people were jammed together, even the aisles were fitted with seats. People were on all sides of him. Anyone who has seen Plymouth Church will realize the point of the following remarks on the psychology of sug-

of the aim and plan to the needs of his congregation is a fundamental principle of Beecher's psychology of public appeal.

Beecher formulated his theory of organization from the successful methods of others and from his own practice. Concerning the structure of a sermon which arises out of the
needs of the congregation, he says:

Much of the effectiveness of a discourse as well as the ease and pleasure of delivering it, depends upon the plan. Let me earnestly caution you
against the sterile, conventional, regulation plans, that are laid down in

gestion. "The next point you should look to is to have your pews as near as
possible to the speaker. A preacher must be a man among men. There is a force
—call it magnetism, or electricity, or what you will—in a man, which is a personal element, and which flows from a speaker, who is en rapport with his audience. This principle should be utilized in the work of preaching. . . . . People
often say, 'Do you not think it is much more inspiring to speak to a large audience than a small one?' No, I say; I can speak just as well to twelve persons as
to a thousand, provided those twelve are crowded around me and close together,
so that they touch each other. But even a thousand people, with four feet space
between every two of them, would be just the same as an empty room. Every
lecturer will understand what I mean, who has ever seen such audiences and addressed them. But crowd your audience together, and you will set them off with
not half the effort. . . . . Brother Day, the son of Old President Day of Yale
College, was one of my right-hand men in founding the Plymouth Church in
Brooklyn; and being a civil engineer, and the church having voted to build, he
went into my study with me to plan the edifice. He asked me what I wanted, in
the first place, and how many people I wanted the church to seat. I told him.
'Very good,' he said; 'and how do you want them located?' 'I want them to sur-
round me, so that they will come up on every side, and behind me, so that I shall
be in the centre of the crowd, and have the people surge all about me.' The result
is, that there is not a better constructed hall in the world for the purposes of
speaking and hearing than Plymouth Church. Charles Dickens, after giving
one of his readings in it, sent me special word not to build any other hall for
speaking; that Plymouth Church was perfect. It is perfect because it was built
on a principle—the principle of social and personal magnetism, which emanates
reciprocally from a speaker and a close throng of hearers. This is perhaps the
most important element of all the external conditions conducive to good and
effective preaching" (*Yale Lectures* [1st ser.], pp. 73, 74). This condition for
rendering an audience suggestible is recognized by W. D. Scott, *The Psychology
of Public Speaking;* E. A. Ross, *Social Psychology*, chap. iii; and by LeBon, *The
Crowd*, chap. iii.

books, and are frequently taught in seminaries. There is no proper plan. It is quietly assumed by the teachers of formal sermonizing that a sermon is to be unfolded from the interior, or from the nature of the truth with which it deals. That this is one of the elements, and often the chief element, that determines the form of the sermon is true; but it is also true, that the object to be gained by preaching a sermon at all will have as much influence in giving it proper plan as will the nature of the truth handled,—perhaps even more. Nay, if but one or the other could be adopted, that habit of working which shapes one's sermons from the necessities of the minds to which it is addressed is the more natural, the safer, and the more effective.[5]

Organization should not be forced upon the material from without. Sonnets may have conventional forms but not sermons. Sonnets are for expression, sermons are for communication, and communication with all its attendant necessities dictates the organization. Sermons are tools. They exist for their purpose.

Sermons are tools; and the business that you have in hand is not the making of sermons, or the preaching of sermons—it is saving men. Let this come up before you so frequently that it shall never be forgotten, that none of these things should gain ascendency over this prime controlling element of your lives, that you are to save men.[6]

In order to save men the maker of a sermon had to be in sympathy with the problems of men. Beecher was so sensitive to the needs of his congregation that frequently he discarded his prepared sermon plan in favor of another that would more closely meet the needs of his people. Mrs. Beecher[7] relates

[5] *Yale Lectures* (1st ser.), p. 218.   [6] *Ibid.*, p. 38.

[7] *Ladies' Home Journal* (May, 1872), p. 4. Another instance of Beecher's abandoning his prepared plan for another is contained in the following anecdote: "One of the reporters of the *Brooklyn Eagle* was sent one Sunday evening a few years ago to report Mr. Beecher's sermon. The discourse was one of singular power, freshness, and force. The reporter was more than charmed and interested. When the service was over he encountered Mr. Beecher at the foot of the pulpit stairs, and knowing the small store he set upon his manuscript notes, asked him if he would be good enough to give them to him, as he desired to preserve

that her husband confided to her that often after he had entered the pulpit he saw someone who was in trouble, or someone who had silently done a most kind and heroic deed. On
such occasions he would lay aside his prepared notes and launch
into an entirely different sermon from the one prepared. Need-
less to say such a practice demanded unusual resourcefulness
and extraordinary inventive powers.

There is a striking bit of testimony from Beecher regarding
his sensitivity to the needs of the congregation in the following:

> Hundreds and hundreds of times, as I rose to pray and glanced at the
> congregation, I could not keep back the tears. There came to my mind
> such a sense of their wants, there were so many hidden sorrows, there
> were so many weights and burdens, there were so many doubts, there
> were so many states of weakness, there was so many dangers, so many
> perils, there were such histories—not world histories, but eternal histories
> —I had such a sense of compassion for them, my soul so longed for them,
> that it seemed to me as if I could scarcely open my mouth to speak for
> them.[8]

One of the major principles in Beecher's rhetorical theory is
this very careful adaptation of the purpose and plan of the
sermon to the needs of the audience.

The plan was not some sacred pattern to be adhered to in the
pulpit in spite of everything. Some preachers[9] will not allow

---

them as an autobiographical prize and as a memento of the sermon. 'Well,' said
the Plymouth Church pastor, as he fluttered over the half-dozen sheets of note-
paper, 'you can have them, but this is not the sermon I preached. I prepared
this sermon intending to use it; but when I got in the pulpit I got to thinking of
another subject and preached upon that" (Thomas W. Knox, *Life and Work of
Henry Ward Beecher* [Cincinnati, Ohio, 1887]), p. 284.

[8] *Yale Lectures* (2d ser.), p. 46.

[9] Louis Brastow (in *Representative Modern Preachers* [New York, 1904],
p. 92), says of Frederick William Robertson: "He permitted nothing to turn him
aside from careful preparation, and he always gave his mind free movement
along the line of an orderly logical plan." On this point see also C. H. Parkhurst,
Pulpit and Pew (Yale University Press, 1913), p. 53.

anything to disturb their predetermined line of attack. Beecher's plans were not rigid but pliant to be molded by the needs of the audience as well as the purpose of the preacher. Now Beecher knew better than anyone else that this following of the minds of his listeners would result in unpolished, disjointed sermons, which would be displeasing to him when he came to read them.[10] But as I have already shown, he wanted to save men, not sermons. The following quotation describes further his own theory and practice:

You do not want an argument for the sake of an argument. You do not want a sermon that is as perfect a machine as a machine can be, unless it *does* something. You want the people; and the shortest and surest way to get them is the best way. When you are preaching a sermon which has been prepared with a great deal of care, and are laying down the truth with forcible arguments, you will often find that you are losing your hold on the attention of your people by continuing in that direction. But coming to a fortunate point, strike out an illustration which arouses and interests them, leave the track of your argument, and never mind what becomes of your elaborate sermon, and you will see the heavy and uninterested eyes lighting up again. "But," you say, "that will make my sermon unsymmetrical." Well, were you called to preach for the sake of the salvation of sermons? Just follow the stream, and use the bait they are biting at, and take no heed of your sermon. You will find it almost impossible to carry forward the demonstration of a truth in one straight course and yet make it real to a general audience. You must vary your method constantly, and at the same time through it all carry the burden of your discourse so that it shall be made clear to the whole of your audience.[11]

In this paragraph we have a splendid example of Beecher's insight into the problems of appealing to the general public. He understood the psychology of public appeal. He knew that

[10] This point is referred to again in the section on Style. John Morley (*The Life of William Ewart Gladstone* [New York, 1903], II, 589), states: "The statesman who makes or dominates crises, who has to rouse and mould the mind of a senate or nation, has something else to think about than the production of literary masterpieces."

[11] *Yale Lectures* (1st ser.), p. 165.

attention is not constant, that it varies. He realized that it made little difference what one said if the audience were inattentive. What, after all, shall it profit a preacher if his sermon be perfectly constructed, if he lose the attention of his audience? Regarding order, in another connection, he said: "What is order as applied to things? It is simply arrangement according to some notion, and disorder is simply arrangement according to some *other* notion."[12] But disorder must never become confusion. The unity of the discourse was always to be maintained. Unity is a cardinal virtue of rhetoric; without it we have chaos. Beecher never, in battling for the attention of his audience, lost sight of his goal. In the following passage Beecher makes fun of the sermon that does not possess unity.

I heard described the other day a style of preaching which was likened to the way they are said to build ships down in Maine. They build them down there by the mile; and when they have an order they cut off so much, round up a stern and a bow, and send it. Thus some sermons seem to have been built by the mile. There seems to be no earthly reason why the preacher should begin in one place rather than another, or why he should stop in one place rather than another.[13]

A sermon should possess a structural unity that is an outgrowth of a close sympathy with the needs of the people addressed. Beecher's method insured variety in unity. Persuasion is the underlying aim of all preaching but sermons take on varying

[12] *Eyes and Ears* (New York, 1862), p. 413. "Among the superstitions of education are those in favor of order. It is not that there is not such thing as order, but that its advocates are bigoted, are narrow and exclusive. It is coolly taken for granted, that if order is good, disorder is bad. If order is Heaven's first law, disorder is at least its second. What is order, as applied to things? It is simply arrangement according to some notion, and disorder is simply arrangement according to some other notion." It is illuminating to compare with this Hugh Blair's statement, "As obscurity, so disorder, too, is very compatible with Grandeur; nay, frequently heightens it" (Lecture III, "Rhetoric and Belles Lettres").

[13] *Yale Lectures* (1st ser.), p. 27.

purposes. Not only should each sermon be varied in its presentation, but the purpose of individual sermons should vary.

Sometimes it is to call men from their sins; sometimes to repress the malign; sometimes to encourage hope in the faint-hearted; sometimes to instruct the understanding; sometimes to broaden men's knowledge, and move them off their prejudices.[14]

Three of the five general ends of public discourse that appear in a discussion of the ends of speaking in textbooks[15] on public discourse are present in this list: to instruct, to actuate, and to impress. It is not the preacher's business ordinarily to convince, as has already been said. Sometimes, as in the "Liverpool Address," the preacher may strive to convince, but usually such speaking is outside the pulpit. On the lecture platform the preacher might entertain, but not in the pulpit. To be sure, portions of Beecher's sermons did entertain, but entertainment was not their controlling purpose.

C

Variety may be obtained by varying the attack on the theme. Beecher gives a list of the possible plans of approach to the discourse.

It is this necessity of adaptation to the innumerable phases of human nature that reacts upon the sermon, and determines the form it shall take. If it were possible never have two plans alike. It may be well, to-day, to preach an intellectual theme by an analytic process; but that is a reason why, on the following Sunday, an intellectual theme should be treated by a synthetic process. If you have preached the truth by the ways of statement and proof, you have then a reason for following it with a sermon that assumes the truth, and appeals directly to the moral consciousness. A didactic sermon is all the stronger if it follows in strong contrast with a sermon to the feelings. If you have preached to-day to

[14] *Ibid.*, p. 41.

[15] For example, see J. M. O'Neill and A. T. Weaver (*Elements of Speech* [New York, 1926]), in which the ends to instruct, to actuate, to convince, to entertain, and to impress are given.

the heart through the imagination, to-morrow you are to preach to the heart through the reason; and so the sermon like the flowers of the field, is to take on innumerable forms of blossoming. When you have finished your sermon, not a man of your congregation should be unable to tell you, distinctly, what you have done; but when you begin a sermon, no man in the congregation ought to be able to tell you what you are going to do. All these cast-iron frames, these stereotyped plans[16] of sermons, are the devices of the Devil, and of those mischievous devils of the pulpit, formality and stupidity.[17]

Just as human nature is endlessly various so will sermons that meet those needs of human nature be varied. Preaching out of sympathy with people will give an "endless diversity and fertility to subjects for sermons." Sometimes he used analysis; at other times he used synthesis. Beecher might take the form of statement and proof for a sermon; sometimes he might choose a didactic sermon; then, he might choose to reach the heart through the imagination; again, he might choose to reach the head through the reason. These are a few of the modes of varying the approach to actuating an audience.

In analyzing a subject Beecher made no attempt to exhaust it. An effective sermon is the joint product of people and preacher.[18] A sermon must suggest more than it expresses.

[16] Beecher is not declaiming against an imaginary evil as will be seen by reading the following: "When I sit down at my desk I go to work organizing my material. Thanks be for William Converse DeWitt, best of instructors in preaching, who compelled me in the early days to grind out homiletic exercises according to an invariant outline. Almost every sermon I have ever preached has followed this recommended pattern: A. *Point of Contact* (Including statement of the Problem); B. *Discussion* (1) Thesis. (2) Antithesis. (3) Synthesis. C. *Application* (usually a one-sentence summary of the sermon)"—Bernard Iddings Bell, "I Write a Sermon," *If I Had Only One Sermon to Prepare* (New York, 1932), pp. 141–42.

[17] *Yale Lectures* (1st ser.), p. 221; the necessity of variety in sermon-making is mentioned by Beecher on pp. 40, 53, 58, 61, 160, 161, 164, 169, 210, 219, 221, 222, and 223.

[18] This characteristic of Beecher's sermons was noted by the president of Emory College, A. G. Haygood: "If we were to take some sentences and para-

A respectable source of failure is conscientious thoroughness. It is true that it is the office of the preacher to furnish thought for his hearers, but it is no less his duty to excite thought. Thus we give thought to breed thought. If, then, a preacher elaborates his theme until it is utterly exhausted, leaving nothing to the imagination and intellect of his hearers, he fails to produce that lively activity in their minds which is one of the best effects of right preaching; they are merely recipients. But under a true preaching the pulpit and the audience should be carrying on the subject together, one in outline, and the other with subtle and rapid activity, filling it up by imagination, suggestion, and emotion. Don't make your sermons too good. That sermon, then, has been overwrought which leaves nothing for the mind of the hearer to do. A sermon in outline is often far more effective than a sermon fully thought out and delivered as a completed thing. Painters often catch the likeness of their subject when they have sketched in the picture only, and paint it out when they are finishing it; and many and many a sermon, if it had been but sketched upon the minds of men, would have conveyed a much better idea of the truth than is produced by its elaborate painting and filling up. This is the secret of what is called "suggestive preaching," and it is also the secret of those sermons which are called "good but heavy."[19]

The artist in Beecher is evident in this statement. The speech, like the painting, does not convey thought and feeling but stirs it up in the audience. As Professor Parker has said:

Only so much of things needs to be represented as is necessary to give back the life to them. Necessary above all is the object as a whole, for to this our feelings are attached; now this can usually be far better represented through an impressionistic sketch, which gives only the significant features, than by a painstaking and detailed drawing.[20]

---

graphs out of their connection, they would be considered heresies. Take the sermon as a whole, and what he did not say that, from our standpoint, was necessary to the statement of complete truth, was implied. The question occurred to us while we listened with charmed ear and deeply moved heart, Does this great congregation bring these grand half-truths together? It is to be hoped they did" (Abbott and Halliday, *Henry Ward Beecher*, p. 402).

[19] *Yale Lectures* (1st ser.), p. 223.

[20] DeWitt H. Parker, *The Principles of Aesthetics* (New York, 1920), p. 266.

The audience fills up the outline suggested by the speaker.[21] As Whately has put it, this type of speaking "puts the hearer's mind into the same *train of thought* as the speaker's, and suggests to him more than is actually expressed."[22]

Others have noticed that the public speaker should suggest trains of thought for the audience to pursue. A sentence from Walt Whitman, for example, on public speaking indicates that he, too, was careful not to overload his lecture. "Do not attempt to put too much in one lecture, nor make it too complicated."[23] Beecher discovered that he could avoid making his sermons too complicated by what he chose to call "the line-of-fact" or "the series-of-parables" form of sermon structure. He could sketch the principal features of his thought by the use of many parables or by a series of statements. Again, this loose type of organization was dictated by the intellectual capacity of his congregation.[24]

Consider how various are the methods by which men receive truths. Most men are feeble in logical power. So far from being benefited by an

[21] Richard Storrs (*Preaching Without Notes* [New York, 1875], p. 23) has commented upon elaborate plans as the cause of failure in speaking without notes. "I saw at a glance what the secret of the failure had been. I had made too much preparation in detail, had written out heads, sub-divisions, even some passages or paragraphs in full, in order that I might be certain beforehand to have material enough at command; and the result of it was that I was all the time looking backward, not forward, in preaching; trying to remember, not only prearranged trains of thought but particular forms of expression, instead of trusting to the impulse of the subject, and seeking to impress certain great and principal features of it on the congregation."

[22] *Elements of Rhetoric*, Part III, chap. ii, sec. 9.

[23] C. J. Furness, *Walt Whitman's Workshop* (Harvard University Press, 1928), p. 36.

[24] Oliver Wendell Holmes (*Autocrat of the Breakfast Table*, p. 140), has commented upon the intellectual capacity of the average audience. "A thoroughly popular lecture ought to have nothing in it which five hundred people cannot take all in a flash, just as it is uttered. But I tell you the *average* intellect of five hundred persons, taken as they come, is not very high. It may be safe and sound so far as it goes, but it is not very rapid or profound."

exact concatenated development of the truth, they are in general utterly unable to follow it. At the second or third step they lose the clew. The greatest number of men, particularly uncultivated people, receive their truth by facts placed in juxtaposition rather than in philosophical sequence. Thus a line of facts or a series of parables will be better adapted to most audiences than a regular unfolding of a train of thought from the germinal point to the fruitful end. The more select portion of an intelligent congregation, on the other hand, sympathize with truth delivered in its highest philosophic forms. There is a distinct pleasure to them in the evolution of an argument. They rejoice to see a structure built up tier upon tier, story upon story. They glow with delight as the chain is welded, link by link. And if the preacher himself be of this mind, and if he receives the commendations of the most thoughtful and cultured of his people, it is quite natural that he should fall wholly under the influence of this style of sermonizing; so he will feed one mouth and starve a hundred.[25]

An examination of Beecher's usual practice discloses the employment of this line-of-fact or series-of-parables form of organization. His popular lectures, "The Reign of the Common People" and "The Wastes and Burdens of Society" reveal a series of topics held together by their thematic relation. The last-named address is, for instance, a series of wastes and burdens, such as the wastes of sickness, of weakness, of parasitic waste, of ignorance, of quarrelsomeness, of misfits, of lying, of drunkenness, of war. It can readily be seen how Beecher's skill in the use of illustrations fitted in so perfectly with this conception of organization.

While rhetoricians generally recognize that uncultivated people respond to emotional appeals more quickly and effectively than to intellectual appeals, and while they recognize that concrete illustrations are more instantly intelligible to the uncultivated than abstract statements, nowhere have I found the formula, *line of fact or series of parables*, advocated by Beecher, similarly expressed elsewhere. F. N. Scott said of

[25] *Yale Lectures* (1st ser.), p. 219. The same thought is expressed in *ibid.*, pp. 157, 160, and 226.

De Quincey: "He discovered capacities of prose, which, before his time, had not been known to exist; or, if they existed in isolation, no one had before woven them together, and to weave together, is, in art, a new thing."[26] Beecher took commonplaces of rhetoric and wove them together into a prescription suitable for a type of discourse intended to reach the common people.

On the other hand, we have evidence in the "Liverpool Address"[27] that Beecher employed other than the line-of-fact or series-of-parables form of organization when occasion demanded. The following paragraph, taken from the "Liverpool Address," might be used to illustrate a textbook on paragraph writing because it unfolds so logically.

> There are two dominant races in modern history. The Germanic and the Romanic races. The Germanic races tend to personal liberty, to a sturdy individualism, to civil and to political liberty. The Romanic race tends to absolutism in government; it is clannish; it loves chieftains; it develops a people that crave strong and showy governments to support and plan for them. The Anglo-Saxon carries self-government and self-development with him wherever he goes. He has popular Government and popular Industry; for the effects of a generous civil liberty are not seen a whit more plain in the good order, in the intelligence, and in the virtue of self-governing people, than in their amazing enterprise and the scope and power of their creative industry. The power to create riches is just as much a part of the Anglo-Saxon virtues as the power to create good order and social safety. The things required for our commerce are three. First, liberty; second, liberty; third, liberty. Though these are not the same liberty as I shall show you.

Such an example as this indicates Beecher's ability to develop his ideas logically. At the same time it shows that he employed the "line of fact" or "series of parables" in his preaching as a

[26] *Essays on Style, Rhetoric, and Language* (Boston, 1893), Introduction, p. xvi.

[27] In the Appendix will be found a complete brief of the "*Liverpool Address*," which will serve to indicate the logical nature of this discourse.

matter of choice, because he felt that it permitted him great liberty in shaping the sermon in the presence of his congregation.

D

Further light may be thrown upon Beecher's theory of organization by an examination of his practice. Fortunately, J. B. Pond, Beecher's lecture manager, includes a photographic copy of the outline of the "Address to Students" in his book, *A Summer in England with Henry Ward Beecher*. The address concerns preaching and its problems, a familiar subject. From an outline of 400 words Beecher constructed a speech of approximately 11,800 words. In comparing the outline and the speech I find that there are many headings in the address that do not appear at all in the outline. These additional phases of the subject demanded treatment as he developed the subject in the presence of his audience. He did not feel constrained to follow strictly his prepared outline. Expanding and contracting the outline was one of the advantages of composing in the presence of the audience. There are subheads in the outline that do not appear in the address. There is an entire page of the outline that is not developed in the address, evidence that when consumed with his subject he gave little heed to his prepared outline.

It appears from a comparison of the outline and address that Beecher depended upon the outline merely as a guide to prompt thought. For example, on the eighth page of his thirty-page address he was on the fourth page of his seven-page outline. This means that there were only three pages of outline left for twenty-three pages of address, and one of the pages of the outline was omitted from the development entirely, so that actually Beecher used only two pages of his outline for twenty-three pages of address. During the opening moments of speak-

Luke 15: 11 —

1. General Remarks — Drift of Parable
to reveal God's nature — in the relation
of a *Restorer* = Must not insist
upon Ministers — or to who are Elders
& Prayer &c —

II *The Departure* =
        (1) It may be conceived, in not
unfavorable light — With right motives
${}^{x\circ}$ (2.) But, here, it implies —
  1. impatience of restraint
  2. filial infidelity,
  3. Selfishness — may undraw — have in off
  4. Far country — geographical put for Moral
                                                    distance.

FIG. 1.—This is a photostatic copy of the outline considered in the study.
It is reduced one-half but it gives an idea of the character of the notes taken by
Beecher into the pulpit. The writing was large enough to be taken in at a single
glance. It gives evidence of the haste with which it was composed.

Deportment for God –

By heedlp, 1. Men take all God's gifts willingly.
Reason & genius: Youth & health: Susceptibility
to all pleasure: Social position: pleasure
business, honor, Daily gifts of Providence

2. With these, hide God: make
his very gifts a substitute for him. Remove
selves far fr. him, by those very things wh.
sh⁰. have kept him near & in mind –

3. Until come into condition, in
wh. God has no perceptible influence, or
relationship — only circumstance

4. It is, in this divested & unguarded
state, that deterioration goes on fast

III

Riotous Living — And Result —

(1) The Joy of dissipation — Limited

    1. by means pecuniary,

    2. by health — or sensibility of nerve

It does not go far. In any term of years gay dissipation does not produce as much joy as virtue & temperate enjoyment.

(2) When he had spent all — Mighty famine. — He began to be in Want

(3) Steps of degradation — threw himself on Others — paid for it by menial work

(4) Suffering a means of teaching Moral Law — Just such Creatures, all about us — Men Vulgarized by Vice — outcast gains. Every living mean way of prolonging misery —

IV. (Repent. & Reformation)

1. _Came to Himself_ — To look his
Case in face & reason on it —

2. Office of _Memory_! "How many kinds &"

   (1) Blessed they, who have youth & family
to remember!

   (2) How bright, & how sad — one meaning
of last joys!

3. _The Resolution_ —

4. The _DECISIVE_ Step — Not, "I will
arise" — but — "_He arose_"

   This settled it —

The Execution of plan — Father's
Heart revealed =

Application

1. Sin carries its own penalties.

2. Repentance & Reformation
open to the worst sinns —
  No other Conditions

  Could there be Gp?

3. God's feeling toward Wrong
Doers —

  (1.) It is sorrow — Anger only in
Sence of Moral indignation —

  (2) The first signs of Return —

  (3) The Joy of God — greater than
of Sinners —

ing, Beecher apparently followed his outline, but as he kindled to his subject he got further and further away from it.[28]

To discover further what we can of Beecher's practice of organization let us consider a typical outline. The following is a typewritten copy of the sermon outline which I found in manuscript in the collection at Plymouth Church, Brooklyn, N.Y.[29]

THE PRODIGAL SON

Luke 15:11

I. General Remarks—Drift of Parable to reveal God's Nature—in the relation of a Restorer—must not insist upon minutiae—as to who are elder and younger.

II. The Departure
   1. It may be conceived in not unfavorable light—with right motives.
   2. But here it implies
      1. Impatience of restraint
      2. Filial infidelity
      3. Selfishness—waywardness—moral indifference
      4. *Far* country—geographical put for moral distance
   3. Departure from God
      1. Men take all God's gifts willingly, Reason and genius; Youth pleasure; susceptibility to all pleasure; Social position; pleasure; business, honor, Daily gifts of Providence.
      2. *With these*, hide God; make his very gifts a substitute for him. —Remove selves far from him by those very things which should have kept him near and in mind.

[28] These observations drawn from objective data are corroborated in Lyman Abbott's description of Beecher's practice in the pulpit. "When the time for the sermon came, the notes lay on the open Bible before him. He read in a quiet manner not always audible throughout the church unless it were notably still, the first and fully written pages, dropped his manuscript to throw in a thought that flashed upon him, came back to it again, presently dropped it altogether, either not to recur to it at all, or to recur to it only to catch from some word or sentence a hint as to the next point in the current thought" (*Henry Ward Beecher*, p. 119).

[29] At this point I wish to express my appreciation to Dr. J. Stanley Durkee for making the Beecher manuscripts at Plymouth Church available to me.

3. Until come into Condition in which God has no perceptible influence, or relationship—only circumstance.
4. It is in this divested and unguarded state, that deterioration goes on fast.

III. Riotous Living and Results
    1. The joy of dissipation—limited
        1. By means pecuniary
        2. By health—or sensibility of nerve. It does not go far. In any term of years gay dissipation does not produce as much joy as virtue and temperate enjoyment
    2. When he had spent all—Mighty famine—He began to be in want.
    3. Steps of degradation—Threw himself on others—paid for it by menial work.
    4. Suffering a means of teaching Moral Law. Just such creatures all about us. Men vulgarized by vice. Outcast by crime. Living memory and prolonging misery.

IV. Repentance and Reformation
    1. Came to Himself to look his case in the face and reason on it.
    2. Office of Memory: How many hired, etc.
        1. Blessed are they who have youth and family to remember.
        2. How bright and how sad are memory of lost joys.
        3. The resolution.
        4. The Decisive Step. Not "I will arise" but "He arose."

 V. The execution of plan—Father's heart revealed.

APPLICATION

1. Sin carries its own penalties
2. Repentance and Reformation open to worst sins
No other condition—
Could there be less—
3. God's feeling toward wrong-doers
    1. It is sorrow; Anger only in sense of moral indignation
    2. The first signs of Return
    3. The joy of God—greater than of sinner.

The foregoing outline reveals much of Beecher's practice in arranging his ideas. It is plain that there is considerable irregularity of form in this outline. The plan is evidently not for publication. Such a plan would be liberally blue-penciled by a teacher of Freshman composition for its failure to observe the decorum of symbols. No attention is paid to whether the thought is represented by a sentence, a phrase, or word. It was jotted down in the strain and stress of creativeness. The divisions might have been better developed on second thought. It will be noticed that the beginning of the outline is much more detailed than the middle or close. It is conceivable that as Beecher kindled to his subject, and saw it opening up before him, he chose not to write down all the details and thus kill inspiration in the pulpit a little later. In the hour before the sermon, he chose the theme of his discourse. During this hour he started the streams of association flowing from the subconscious which would be more fully developed later under the "more than usual state of emotion," to use Coleridge's phrase, as he stood before his congregation. It is likely also that the time factor had something to do with the less developed middle and close. Notice that the fifth point is not developed in the outline at all. To insure, it seems, the trend of thought in the application, Beecher spent some time on it. In the hour before his sermon, Beecher set the stage so that the principals—the speaker, the audience and the occasion could enact the drama of the day.

The sermon is divided into exposition and application. The exposition consists of five large heads: (1) The Departure; (2) Riotous Living; (3) Repentance and Reformation; (4) The Execution of the Father's Plan; (5) Father's heart Revealed. The first four views of the subject have four subdivisions each. (The fifth might have possessed four also had there been time.) The five views coincide with the main episodes of the biblical narrative. They are obvious divisions and could be followed with ease by an audience already familiar with the parable. It should be noticed that no illustrations are indicated: they are left to the moment of speaking. There are three main views in the application. These are not developed to any extent. It looks as if they were jotted down in haste. He spent more time upon his last point, which he evidently meant to make his conclusion, and which is, in fact, the theme of the parable of the Prodigal Son.[30]

It will be interesting and informing to compare one of Spurgeon's outlines with the foregoing discussion. Spurgeon's immediate preparation, as I have shown, was similar to Beecher's. The following are the notes for a sermon, "The Beauty of the Olive Tree," preached April 17, 1879.

Hos. 14:6

Our sojourn among the olives has made us learn their beauty.

I. *It is a kind which grows upon you*
Not seen at once
Seen when the sun glances through them
Seen when forests of them clothe the landscape

II. *A Beauty of the sober kind*
Not that of the golden orange or lemon, or shapely pine
Not that of gay flowers, but seriously glad
The gay cannot enjoy it
Christian serious in his joys

III. *Ever-abiding*
It casts not its leaves. It knows no naked winter

IV. *Ever varied with the seasons*
Its pendent branches, profuse flowers, brown berries
Varying too with light and shade
David thus changeful and all believers

[30] An interesting bit of Beecher's practice which throws additional light upon his outlining occurs in the following: "He habitually limited himself to an hour in preaching, and as the hand of the clock approached that period made haste to a conclusion, which was usually, in obedience to oratorical instinct a true peroration in form" (Rossiter W. Raymond, *The Crown of Life* [New York, 1890], Introduction).

V. *Individuality*
No two alike. No one which is not a study
Young and old, twisted in a thousand forms

VI. *Life—struggling, historic beauty*
Its roots, its boughs, its gnarls and roots
Its bosses of fatness. Its white head

VII. *Its fruitfulness*
Best of crops. Food, light, medicine
Joy, peace

VIII. *Its progeny*
The young olives around it

IX. *Its lopping and after greenness*

X. *Its reminding you of the Lord.*[31]

It will be recalled that Beecher theorized that large congregations of the common people could follow a line of facts. Spurgeon's outline is composed of many facts about the olive tree. The whole sermon is undoubtedly intended to be a parable. Thus, Spurgeon employs the formula put forth by Beecher for reaching large assemblies of common people, whom Spurgeon likewise attracted.

By studying the outline it can be seen that it, too, is much fuller at the beginning than at the close. Spurgeon, like Beecher, when he felt sure of his line of development, did not think it necessary to put it down on paper.[32] It will be noticed also that

[31] A photographic copy of this outline faces page 208 in W. Y. Fullerton's *C. H. Spurgeon, A Biography* (London, 1920).

[32] The same practice carried to an extreme is seen in the following testimony. "My preaching is done with a minimum of explicit preparation. I never write a sermon before its delivery, and I do not even prepare an outline in notes. I began sixteen years ago by using a full manuscript. Then I tried memorizing the manuscript. Then I reduced myself to the preparation of a very complete outline which I used in preaching. Then I abandoned the use of notes in the pulpit, but kept on making the outline in preparation. Then I cut down the outline to a few lines. Then—I awoke to the fact that I did not need any *paper* preparation. My mind had accustomed itself to the process of what might be called subconscious structural preparation. So now I go into the pulpit charged

the form of the sermon is irregular as in Beecher's case. The outline is not divided into two parts, exposition and application: the application is made as the preacher proceeds, i.e., "Christian serious in his joys," occurs under point two.

Beecher's theory of sermon planning was an integral part of his theory of extempore speaking. That speaking is best, Beecher theorized, that most adequately meets the needs of the audience. Planning that is made independent of these needs is impotent. Effective sermon plans are evolved in the presence of the audience. Unity of effect is not to be sacrificed. Variety in unity is requisite for holding attention. Beecher's emphasis on suggestive preaching reveals an understanding of the aesthetic values in the speaking situation. In stating that common people in large congregations are reached by the line-of-fact or series-of-parables form of organization, Beecher is adding to our knowledge of the instruments of persuasion. Beecher's practice bears out his theory of loose organization evolved in the presence of the audience. Beecher's remarks on the disposition of material constitute an attempt to construct a theory of organization for extempore speaking.

---

with the thought and the feeling of the hour and of the subject, and let the preaching take care of itself. So habituated have I become to this method, that any other merely handicaps my style, my delivery, and the flow of thought into language. Nor have I sacrificed one whit of my style or my diction to this method. You understand, of course, however, that such a technique requires as much *actual*—if not explicit—preparation as would the preparation of a fully written and memorized sermon. One's preparation for preaching becomes like one's breathing or his heartbeat. And when I enter the pulpit, while I have no certain idea as to exactly the form which my sermon will take, I am completely certain what chief points I shall be making and what end I shall reach. I am full of the subject, and all overflowing with it, keen to speak it out, familiar with its motifs and acquainted with its harmonies of mental development. So that, if the method be that of extempore speaking, the spirit is that of most thoroughly matured thought." The Rev. Dwight Bradley, "Sermon Psychology," *If I Had Only One Sermon To Prepare* (New York, 1932), p. 171.

STYLE

A. Words and idioms
1. Words and action
2. Symbolic nature of words
3. Anglo-Saxon words
4. Everyday idioms
5. Grammar
6. Vocabulary
7. The adjective

B. The sentence
1. Vernacular
2. Rhythmical
3. Length

C. Qualities
1. Common
2. Clearness

D. Concepts
1. Embodying the thought
2. Personal expression
3. Effective expression

A

The necessity of moving an audience to action influenced Beecher's thinking on the matter of style. Since words are the seeds of action, he was vitally interested in their changing values. A preacher must be a man of words if he is to persuade man to turn from evil to good. Beecher remarked: "People say, 'Show me a man of deeds, and not of words.' You might as well say, 'Show me a field of corn; I don't care about clouds and rain.' Talking makes thought and feeling, and thought and feeling make action. Show me a man of words who knows how to incite noble deeds."[1] This close relationship of language

[1] *Yale Lectures* (1st ser.), p. 189.

to thought, and thought to action has been remarked upon by
Emerson in a passage that is strikingly similar to Beecher's.
Emerson said, "Words and deeds are quite indifferent modes
of the divine energy. Words are also actions and actions are a
kind of words."[2] Because words have the power to provoke action, it is essential that the speaker have at command the right
word.[3] Even the right word leaves a gap between the thought
and the expression, between the ideal and the real. Beecher
was aware of the "sad incompetence of speech,"[4] as Wordsworth put it. Thought is only inadequately represented by
words. Thought is too deep for words. Picturesquely, Beecher
expresses their incompetence and impotence. "Words are but
the bannerets of a great army; thoughts are the main body as
it moves. Words show here and there a gleam in the air, but
the great multitude of thoughts march unseen below."[5] And
yet, the speaker must do the best he can with these words,
along with gestures,[6] to arouse in the minds of his audience the
counterpart of the pattern that exists in his mind. Beecher

[2] *The Poet.* The *Auction Sale Catalogue* lists the following collection of Emerson's works: *Parnassus, Letters and Social Aims, Conduct of Life, Representative
Men, Essays, Poems,* etc., 8 vols., 16 mo and 12mo cloth (Boston, 1850–84). (Includes two copies of the first edition of *Conduct of Life* and *Parnassus,* 12mo,
cloth [Boston, 1875]).

[3] Beecher had to choose his words when in England. "I had to speak extempore on subjects the most delicate and difficult as between our two nations,
where even the shading of my words was of importance" (Harriet Beecher Stowe,
Men of Our Times, p. 560).

[4] *The Prelude,* Book VI, lines 592–94 (Boston, 1888).

[5] *A Treasury of Illustration* (New York, 1904), sec. 2442.

[6] The speaker has an advantage over the writer in that he has gesture to aid
him in stirring up thought in the minds of his audience. Beecher recognizes the
importance of delivery but offers no suggestions as to training the speaker to
have an effective delivery. He says relative to the importance of posture and
gesture in speaking: "A man's whole form is a part of his public speaking. His
feet speak and so do his hands" (*Yale Lectures* [1st ser.], p. 71). In his "Lecture
on Oratory," he says: "At times there are no gestures that are comparable to the
simple stature of the man himself. Frequently the foot is emphasis, and the

knew that words are only effective as they have the ability to
stir up trains of thought in the auditor's mind. Beecher asked
apropos of the symbolic nature of words, "Do you think that
words, in and of themselves, have any signification? Words
mean whatever they have the power to make us think when we
look at them. The Bible cannot contain truth. God does not
live in a book."[7] Thought lives in the minds of men and is only
represented by the word.[8] The speaker must be aware of the
power of words to provoke the thought he desires. Not all
words have this power in the same degree.[9] The speaker will
find, Beecher believed, that effective, association-provoking
words, are largely Anglo-Saxon in origin; he will also discover

posture is oftentimes power after a word, or accompanying a word; and men
learn to perceive the thought coming afar off from the man himself who fore-
shadows it by his action. What power there is in posture or in gesture! By it
how many discriminations are made; how many smooth things are rolled off;
how many complex things men are made to comprehend! how many things the
body can tongue when the tongue itself cannot well utter the thing desired."

[7] *Norwood* (New York, 1866), p. 55; the symbolic nature of words was expressed many times by Beecher. For example, in *Eyes and Ears*, p. 187; in
Treasury of Illustration, secs. 2054, 2299, 2442, and 2576.

[8] Beecher was acquainted with George Campbell's excellent discussion of
"The Nature and Power of Signs, both in Speaking and in Thinking," *The Philosophy of Rhetoric*, Book II, chap. vii, sec. 1. "But the connection that sub-
sisteth between words and things is in its origin arbitrary. Yet the difference in
the effect is not so considerable as one would be apt to imagine. In neither case
is it the matter, if I may be allowed the expression, but the power of the sign that
is regarded by the mind." Beecher knew also Samuel P. Newman's chapter on
"Skill in the Use of Language," which takes up the symbolic nature of language
(*Practical System of Rhetoric* [New York, 1834], p. 117). There is also an excellent discussion on the symbolic nature of language in John Locke's "Essay Concerning Human Understanding" (*Language and Its Proper Use*), with which
Beecher was no doubt familiar.

[9] C. K. Ogden and I. A. Richards, *The Meaning of Meaning* (New York,
1927), p. 11: "Between a thought and a symbol causal relations hold. When
we speak the symbolism we employ is caused partly by the reference we are
making and partly by social and psychological factors—the purpose for which
we are making the reference, the proposed effect of our symbols, and our own
attitude."

that the idioms of everyday speech are his best allies in his fight for attention and action.

Every man ought to know the charm there is in using vernacular and idiomatic phrases. I have known a great many most admirable preachers who lost almost all real sympathetic hold upon their congregations because they were too literary, too periphrastic, and too scholastic in their diction. They always preferred to use large language, rather than good Anglo-Saxon English. But let me tell you there is a subtle charm in the use of plain language that pleases the people. It gives bell-notes which ring out suggestions to the popular heart. There are words that men have heard when boys at home, around the hearth and the table, words that are full of father and mother, and full of common and domestic life. These are the words that afterward, when brought into your sermon, will produce a strong influence on your auditors, giving an element of success; words which will have an effect that your hearers themselves cannot understand. For after all, simple language is loaded down and stained through with the best testimonies of life![10]

How similar this thought is to the advice of Herbert Spencer on the use of language can best be judged after reading the following from Spencer's *The Philosophy of Style*, which Beecher regarded very highly as has been shown.[11] The thought is also identical with that expressed by Whately[12] which Beecher also studied, and which Spencer[13] likewise knew.

[10] *Yale Lectures* (1st ser.), p. 131; a like passage also occurs on p. 231.

[11] *Supra.*, p. 15.

[12] Whately, *Elements of Rhetoric*, Part III, chap. i, Sec. 2: "It is not necessary to dwell on that obvious rule laid down by Aristotle, to avoid uncommon, and, as they are vulgarly called, *hard* words, i.e., those which are such to the persons addressed; but it may be worth remarking, that to those who wish to be understood by the lower orders of the English, one of the best principles of selection is to prefer terms of *Saxon* origin, which will generally be more familiar to them, than those derived from the Latin (either directly, or through the medium of the French), even when the latter are more in use among persons of education. (A remarkable instance of this is, that while the children of the higher classes almost always call their parents 'Papa!' and 'Mama!' the children of the peasantry usually call them by the title of 'Father!' and 'Mother!')"

[13] Spencer's essay on "The Philosophy of Style" appeared originally in the *Westminster Review* for October, 1852, as a review article upon Whately's *Ele-*

The greater forcibleness of Saxon English or rather non-Latin English, first claims our attention. The several special reasons assignable for this may all be reduced to the general reason—economy. The most important of them is early association. A child's vocabulary is almost wholly Saxon. He says, I *have*, not I *possess;* I *wish*, not I *desire;* he does not *reflect*, he *thinks;* he does not beg for *amusement*, but for *play;* he calls things *nice* or *nasty*, not *pleasant* or *disagreeable.* The synonyms which he learns in after years, never become so closely, so organically connected with the ideas signified, as do these original words used in childhood; and hence the association remains less strong. But in what does a strong association between a word and idea differ from a weak one? Simply in the greater ease and rapidity of suggestive action. It can be in nothing else. Both of two words, if they be strictly synonymous, eventually call up the same image.[14]

Both Beecher and Spencer were aware of the fact that the words of everyday experience, the words learned early in life, the Saxon words, are saturated with experience, and go quickest to the mark. It is these everyday expressions that lend vigor to a speaker's style. The same thought is expressed by Emerson regarding the power of everyday words.

The language of the street is always strong. What can describe the folly and emptiness of scolding like the word *jawing?* I feel the force of the double negative, though clean contrary to our grammar rules. And I confess to some pleasure from the stinging rhetoric of a rattling oath in the mouth of truckmen and teamsters. How laconic and brisk it is by the side of a page of the *North American Review.* Cut these words and they would bleed; they are vascular and alive; they walk and they run. Moreover, they who speak them have this elegancy, that they do not trip in their speech. It is a shower of bullets, whilst Cambridge and Yale men correct themselves and begin again at every half sentence.[15]

Emerson has noted, as did Beecher, that the choice of everyday expressions gives a charm to one's speech that is obtain-

---

ments of *Rhetoric*, edited by J. W. Parker, Blair's *Lectures on Rhetoric and Belles Lettres*, Campbell's *Philosophy of Rhetoric*, and Lord Kames's *Elements of Rhetoric.*

[14] *Philosophy of Style*, ed. F. N. Scott, p. 5.

[15] *The Heart of Emerson's Journals*, ed. Bliss Perry (New York, 1909), p. 154.

able in no other way. Beecher, in advocating the use of the vernacular, is not only in harmony with such writers as Herbert Spencer and Emerson, but he is a harbinger of the present-day movement toward the teaching of the use of the common words and idioms of everyday life.[16] This movement is a rebellion against the former attitude that discouraged the use of vernacular and colloquial words.

In the quotation from Emerson there is a reference to the occasional effectiveness of the ungrammatical. Beecher did not scruple at the powerful, though ungrammatical, phrase. Grammar was always a secondary consideration with him. Beecher's defiance of grammar, "Young man when the English language gets in my way, it doesn't stand a chance," has been given wide circulation by George Herbert Palmer in his *Self-Cultivation in English.* Beecher's position regarding grammar is summed up in the sentence, "The moment your grammar and your literature are a stronger relish to you than the substance of your thought or the feeling of an honest man, that very moment there is mischief in the room."[17] It is true of Beecher as Walter Raleigh said of Shakespeare, "He breaks through grammar only to get nearer the heart of things."[18] There is a good example of Beecher's using the vernacular in the following quotation from T. P. O'Connor:

[16] Professor F. N. Scott has written an interesting essay on attempts to ridicule new words and phrases, called *"Verbal Taboos"* (*The Standard of American Speech and Other Papers*, p. 165); perhaps Professor Scott received his suggestion from Coleridge, who, in *Literary Remains*, II, 273, said, "It would form an interesting essay, or rather series of essays, in a periodical work, were all the attempts to ridicule new phrases brought together, the proportion observed of the words ridiculed which have been adopted, and are now common." T. E. Rankin, C. D. Thorpe, M. Solve (*College Composition* [New York, 1929]) said: "The idiom gives a ruggedness and flavor to writing that cannot be achieved by other means. It sometimes appears that grammar is a foe to idiom, but in such cases grammar should go."

[17] *Yale Lectures* (1st ser.), p. 99; also, p. 66.

[18] Walter Raleigh, *Shakespeare* (London, 1924), p. 225.

One of the strong impressions is the way Beecher spoke of a man as 'bought.' In that single word 'bought' he managed to convey such a wealth of meaning that you could see his soul rising and getting his whole nation to rise against that corruption which was then so terrible a feature of the life of so many cities of America.[19]

It is impossible to record here all the interesting phrases found in Beecher's sermons and lectures. Perhaps a few will suffice. Professor John Earle[20] says he first found the phrase *at that*, which he terms an Americanism, in the sermons of Henry Ward Beecher. The word *hellion*, H. L. Mencken[21] records he found in the sermons of Henry Ward Beecher, and terms it a contribution to the American language from the backwoods pulpit. Beecher uses the word *slime* as a verb and interestingly enough Keats uses the word as a verb.[22] A few of the vernacular phrases that flavor Beecher's style are—*to set-off an audience, to turn up one's nose, to make a man cotton to you*,[23] *to cuff about the controversies of theology*.[24] Many of the idioms found in Beecher are still current in the speech of today; others have passed out of use.

Beecher was always on the look-out for telling words and phrases. He sought them not only in the street but in the library. He set out deliberately to enlarge his vocabulary and he advised the young preachers at Yale to do the same.

[19] T. P. O'Connor, M.P., "Orators Who Have Influenced Me," *Harper's Weekly* (September, 1913), p. 10.

[20] *English Prose* (London, 1890), p. 301.

[21] *The American Language* (New York, 1923), p. 94.

[22] Beecher says, "The man who *slimes* his way with the worm, etc." The line from Keats is, "Speak not of grief, young stranger, or grief will *slime* the rose to-night" (*Endymion*, Book IV).

[23] J. S. Fraser and W. E. Henley tell us (in *Slang and Its Analogies* [London, 1791], p. 108) concerning *cotton to:* "To take a fancy to; to unite with; to agree with"; in the last sense it is found occasionally in Elizabethan writers, and is American by survival.

[24] J. O. Halliwell, *A Dictionary of Archaic and Provincial Words* (London, 1890), p. 285. *To cuff* means to dilate.

It is desirable that the preacher should have a copious vocabulary, and a facility in the selection and use of words; and to this end he should read much, giving attention to the words and phrases used by the best authors, not for servile copying and memorizing, but that these elements may become assimilated with his own mind, as a part of it, ready for use when the time comes.[25]

Beecher evidently practiced what he preached. Rossiter W. Raymond tells us that frequently he found Beecher reading with apparent zest (in this case not the best authors, however!) essays or romances which no critic would place in the first rank. "How can you bear such turgid 'fine writing?' " Raymond asked. "It's a gorgeous vocabulary," Beecher replied, "and I want it."[26] Words rushed to Beecher's aid when he stood composing in the presence of his audience. In the vehemence of extempore speech, words jostled each other. "Words," he declared one day, "When I am well started, I don't need to hunt for words! They come in crowds, getting in one another's way, and each one saying, 'Take me! take me!' "[27] Other literary workers make it a practice to stalk words. Emerson relates that he found Barrow a fertile hunting ground for "vigorous phrases and quaint, peculiar words."[28]

Interestingly enough, Barrow was also studied by Beecher in the interest of his own language development. It was from Barrow that Beecher gained his sense of the power of adjectives. Beecher states:

Ordinarily, adjectives are the parasites of substantives—courtiers that hide or smother the king with blandishments—but in Barrow's hands they

[25] *Yale Lectures* (1st ser.), p. 228.

[26] *The Crown of Life* (New York, 1890), Introduction.   [27] *Ibid.*

[28] *The Heart of Emerson's Journals*, ed. Bliss Perry (New York, 1909): "Have been reading patches of Barrows and Ben Johnson; and what the object—not curiosity? No—nor expectation of edification, intellectual or moral—but merely because they are the authors where vigorous phrases and quaint, peculiar words and expressions may be sought and found, the better 'to rattle out the battle of my thoughts.' "

become useful and indeed quite a respectful element of composition. Considering my early partiality for Barrow, I have always regarded it as a wonder that I escaped so largely from the snares and temptations of that rhetorical demon, the adjective.[29]

The adjective, Beecher realized, is the enemy of the noun, as someone as aptly said. When too many adjectives are used, or when too powerful an adjective is employed, the effect of the noun is compromised.

B

Words mean one thing when standing alone and something else when related to other words in phrases and sentences. Words act and react on each other. Words should not only be carefully selected but their combinations should be skilfully effected. "Sometimes a single word," Beecher declared, "like a drop of ink in a tumbler of water, will change the color of a whole statement."[30] Preaching that takes its inspiration from the needs of men and their daily goings and comings, preaching that seeks action, not praise for its beauty, will have its effect upon sentence structure as well as upon the preacher's choice of words. "Show sermons" or "great sermons"[31] had no place in the kind of preaching Beecher was describing. A sermon's greatness depends upon its effect in transforming the lives of the people to whom it is addressed, not in constructing "permanent literary expression," to use a phrase employed by Brewster[32] to designate one of the five common concepts of style. This matter will receive more attention when I come to discuss Beecher's definition of style.

Sentences in Beecher's conception of preaching have work to do. They are impelled by a purpose. They grow independ-

---

[29] Preface to *Lectures to Young Men* (New York, 1845).

[30] *Eyes and Ears* (Boston, 1862), p. 403.

[31] *Yale Lectures* (1st ser.), p. 31; the same thought is also expressed on p. 227.

[32] W. T. Brewster, *Representative Essays on Style* (New York, 1905), p. xiv.

ent of any preconceived plan. They unfold in the presence of
the audience. They must be concerned with utility and whatever beauty arises will be the beauty of a task completed. As in
conversation we are inattentive to our sentence patterns so we
should be in our public speaking. Our thought, not our form,
should be our concern.

The effect of this notion of preaching—a preaching from sympathy
with living men rather than from sympathy with any particular system of
thought—upon the preacher's style will be very great. I have often heard
ministers in private conversation and said, "Would to God you would do
so in the pulpit!" But the moment they are in the pulpit they fall into
their scholastic, artificial style, which runs through the whole ministerial
life. A man will stop you in the street and discourse with you there, and
be just as limber and affable in his sentences, just as curt and direct and
crisp and simple in conversational vernacular as any one; and yet in the
pulpit, two-thirds of what he has to say will be Latin periphrases woven
together; three members on one side the sentence pivot, balanced by three
members on the other, and that recurring all the time. This style is false
to everything but books. It may be all in sympathy with them; but no
man in earnest, talking to his fellow-men with a purpose, falls into that
artificial style.[33]

In this paragraph we have comment on the same kind of
forward-looking element in sentences for extempore speaking
that occurs in De Quincey's contrast of the style of Burke and
Dr. Johnson.[34] The thought of Beecher and De Quincey is so
much alike in this particular as instantly to challenge comparison. De Quincey writes:

We may take the opportunity of noticing what it is that constitutes
the peculiar and characterizing circumstances in Burke's manner of com-

[33] *Yale Lectures* (1st ser.), p. 43.

[34] It might be interesting here to note Beecher's remark on Dr. Johnson's
style: "As an instance of contrasted style, let one read the immortal allegory of
John Bunyan in contrast with the grandiose essays of Dr. Johnson. Bunyan is
to-day like a tree planted by the rivers of water, that bringeth forth his fruit
in season; his leaf shall not wither. Johnson, with all his glory, lies like an Egyp-
tian king, buried and forgotten in the pyramid of his fame" (*Yale Lectures* [1st
ser.], p. 231).

position. It is this: that under his treatment every truth, be it what it may, every thesis of a sentence *grows* in the very act of unfolding it. Take any sentence you please from Dr. Johnson, suppose, and it it will be found to contain a thought, good or bad, fully preconceived. Whereas in Burke, whatever may have been the preconception, it receives a new determination or inflexion at every clause of the sentence. Some collateral adjunct of the main proposition, some temperament or restraint, some oblique glance at its remote affinities, will invariably be found to attend the progress of his sentences, like the spray from a waterfall or the scintillations from the iron under the blacksmith's hammer. Hence, whilst a writer of Dr. Johnson's class seems only to look back upon his thoughts, Burke looks forward, and does in fact advance and change his own station concurrently with the advance of the sentences. This peculiarity is no doubt in some degree due to the habit of extempore speaking, but not to that only.[35]

The difference noted here by De Quincey[36] is one of the essential dissimilarities in the use of the sentence by the speaker and the writer. The writer is thinking with a pen in his hand and the speaker is thinking on his feet in the presence of an audience. The writer focuses his attention on the sentence patterns he is weaving; the speaker focuses his attention on the thought he is bringing to bear upon the audience. The writer looks backward in order to polish his sentences; the speaker looks forward in order to persuade his audience.

There is only one other passage in Beecher's works that mentions the nature of the structure of sentences. The artificial structure of sentences is again disparaged; and the rhythmical quality and length of sentences are considered.

He should also have an ear for strong and terse, but rhythmical sentences which flow without jolt and jar. Above all other men, the preacher should avoid what may be called a literary style, as distinguished from a

[35] Thomas De Quincey, *Essays on Style, Rhetoric and Language,* ed. F. N. Scott (Boston, 1893), p. 185, n.

[36] The *Auction Sale Catalogue* lists the following works of De Quincey: *Narrative and Miscellaneous Papers, Autobiographic Sketches,* and *Miscellaneous Essays,* 4 vols., 12 mo (Boston, 1854–55).

natural one; and by a "literary style" technically so called, I understand one in which abound these two elements—the artificial structure of sentences, and the use of words and phrases peculiar to literature alone, and not to common life. Involved sentences, crooked, circuitous and parenthetical, no matter how musically they may be balanced, are prejudicial to a facile understanding of the truth. Never be grandiloquent when you want to drive home a searching truth. Don't whip with a switch that has leaves on if you want to tingle. . . . . It is a foolish and unwise ambition to introduce periphrastic or purely literary terms where they can possibly be avoided. Go right ahead. Don't run around for your meaning. Long sentences may be good, but not twisting ones.[37]

The sentence must have unimpeded movement, must be free from the incubus of preconceived patterns. The other two characteristics, rhythm and length, are barely mentioned. Unfortunately, Beecher does not tell us how the rhythmical effects are to be produced, but this is just another instance of the general rather than specific nature of the *Yale Lectures*. One should train one's ear to detect strong, terse, rhythmical sentences, that is all that is said. The rhythm of prose is an illusive quality, difficult to analyze.[38] It is a problem for the literary worker not a preacher. The task was declared impossible by Robert Louis Stevenson; after stating that it is impossible to find the secret of the rhythm of poetry, he states that the rhythm of prose is even more inexplicable.

Beecher implies, I think, that the rhythm of oral discourse is not the rhythm of written discourse. That such a difference exists, at least between free verse and oral discourse, has been noted by Walt Whitman, who, as a young man, looked forward

[37] *Yale Lectures* (1st ser.), p. 229.

[38] Many attempts have been made to analyze the rhythm of prose. Professor F. N. Scott has a study in rhythm called "The Scansion of Prose Rhythm" in *The Standard of American Speech and Other Papers* (New York, 1926); also, Dr. W. M. Parrish has an article on "The Rhythm of Oratorical Prose" in *Studies in Rhetoric and Public Speaking in Honor of James Albert Winans* (New York, 1926), pp. 217–31.

to the platform as a means of livelihood.[39] Throughout his life, Whitman never lost his interest in public speaking and its problems. The following passage, in which rhythm is considered, issues from his experience as a public speaker.

The trouble in lecture style is often the endeavor (from the habit of forming the rhythmic style of *Leaves of Grass*) involuntarily to preserve a sort of rhythm in the Lecture sentences—it seems to me this rhythm, for them, is not only not necessary, but is often dangerous to their character requirements—which, for speaking purposes, need to be abrupt, sometimes crackling, with strong contrasts.[40]

Beecher's *strong and terse* is similar to Whitman's *abrupt* and sometimes *crackling*. Beecher's remarks on rhythm are, to say the least, inadequate, yet his practice illustrates an ability to carry out his general ideal. The following sentence illustrates the very thing it preaches: "He should also have an ear for strong and terse, but rhythmical sentences, which flow without jolt and jar." There are some beautiful examples of rhythmical prose in his oration on the death of Lincoln.

In addition to being rhythmical, sentences in oral discourse should be direct. Empirically, Beecher stated a truth about the length of sentences in oral discourse that has recently been verified by Dr. Gladys Borchers,[41] whose study showed that there are only 5,802 chances in 10,000 that the sentence in written style will contain more words than the sentence in oral style. The oral style does not demand short sentences but it does require that the sentence be instantly intelligible by not being "circuitous, parenthetical or involved." Beecher's advice on the necessity of making sentences direct is reasonable. Walter Pater may indulge in involved sentence structure be-

[39] C. J. Furness, *Walt Whitman's Workshop* (Harvard University Press, 1928), p. 28.

[40] *Ibid.*, p. 35.

[41] *A Study of Oral Style* (University of Wisconsin Ph.D. thesis, 1926).

cause he is dealing with the reader who can retrace.[42] In the interest of perspicuity the public speaker should see to it that the clue of the sentences is always apparent, as Whately has said:

In respect to the Construction of Sentences, it is an obvious caution to abstain from such as are too long; but it is a mistake to suppose that the obscurity of many long sentences depends on their length alone. A well-constructed sentence of very considerable length may be more readily understood than a shorter· one which is more awkwardly framed. If a sentence be so constructed that the meaning of each part can be taken in as we proceed (though it be evident that the sense is not brought to a close), its length will be little or no impediment to perspicuity; but if the former part of the sentence convey no distinct meaning till we arrive nearly at the end (however plain it may then appear), it will be, on the whole, deficient in perspicuity; for it will need to be read over, or *thought over*, a second time, in order to be fully comprehended; which is what few readers or hearers are willing to be burdened with.[43]

Both Beecher and Whately were concerned with the economy of the listener's attention. It is true of the other structural elements of style mentioned by Beecher, as it is true of his remarks on the length of the sentence, that he adds nothing to our understanding of style but it is worth while to point out, however, that in such matters as the symbolic character of words, the choice of words, the use of idiomatic phrases, and the rhythm and length of sentences, his views coincide in a remarkable way with the accepted views of those distinguished in literary pursuits.

C

We shall find that in the treatment of the qualities of style, Beecher is as brief and as conventional as he was in the consideration of the structual elements of style. The qualities of an

[42] Cf. Lionel Crocker, "The Voice Element in Prose," *Quarterly Journal of Speech Education* (April, 1926), pp. 168–75.

[43] *Elements of Rhetoric*, Part III, chap. i, sec. 3, pp. 305, 306.

effective style mentioned, but not discussed, by Beecher are such familiar ones as simplicity, fulness, grace, ease, accuracy, and purity. It is easy to show that these qualities have long been used to designate an effective style. Whately, whom I have quoted on the length of sentences above, discusses the problems of style under three heads, perspicuity, elegance, and energy. Most of these qualities enumerated by Beecher come up for consideration in Whately's[44] discussion. *Fulness* is opposed to overconciseness; Whately calls the quality *fulness* "copiousness" which, on the other hand, must not lead to verbosity. Simplicity, grace, and ease help the speaker to obtain elegance. If we turn to Hugh Blair[45] we find that he uses the term "accuracy" in discussing perspicuity. Aristotle[46] designates *purity* as one of the first requisites of an effective style. Beecher does not enter into any discussion of these qualities. They are, in fact, common qualities used to designate an effective style handed down from one rhetorician to another. It would lead me too far afield to attempt to illustrate each one of these qualities from Beecher's works. However, it will be seen that most of these qualities, besides others, are contained in the following passage, taken from the "London Address," which is worthy to occupy a place alongside the most eloquent passages in the English language, as Oliver Wendell Holmes has said.

Standing by my cradle, standing by my hearth, standing by the altar of the church, standing by all the places that mark the name and memory of heroic men who poured their blood and lives for principle, I declare that in ten or twenty years of war we will sacrifice everything we have for principle. If the love of popular liberty is dead in Great Britain, you will not understand us; but if the love of liberty lives as it once lived, and has worthy successors of those renowned men that were our own ancestors as much as yours, and whose example and principles we inherit to make

[44] *Elements of Rhetoric*, Part III.

[45] *Lectures on Rhetoric and Belles Lettres*, Lecture X.

[46] *Rhetoric* III. v.

fruitful as so much seed-corn in a new and fertile land, then you will understand our firm, invincible determination—*to fight this war through*, at all hazards and at every cost.

The only quality of style that gets more than passing mention is that of clearness, one of the virtues of diction mentioned by Aristotle, and always the first to be treated by rhetoricians when discussing the qualities of style. Beecher advised in one of his letters to a son away at college, "Leave nothing merely hinted and left to the reader to make out as best he can."[47] In the *Yale Lectures*, Beecher again touches on the economy of the auditor's attention. He says:

I know some men, among whom, I think, was Coleridge,[48] who justify the obscurities of their style, saying that is a good practice for men to be obliged to dig for the ideas they get. But I submit to you that working on Sunday is not proper for ordinary people in church, and obliging your parishioners to dig and delve for ideas in your sermon is making them do the very work you are paid a salary to do for them.[49]

This reference to Coleridge[50] is undoubtedly to the passage in which the poetry of Milton is being discussed. The reader has

[47] W. C. Beecher, S. Scoville, and Mrs. Henry Ward Beecher, *Life and Letters of Henry Ward Beecher* (New York, 1888), p. 644.

[48] Beecher made this reference to Coleridge in 1872; in 1880, he again mentions Coleridge's thought along with that of Herbert Spencer's: "First among these Herbert Spencer places this: that it is to be done with the least possible labor to the person receiving the idea; and in this respect he is directly opposed to Coleridge, who puts forward the theory that a man who has to dig for knowledge gets more benefit than one who acquires it without the trouble of digging" (Lyman Abbott, ed., *Hints for Home Reading* [New York, 1880], p. 53).

[49] *Yale Lectures* (1st ser.), p. 156.

[50] The *Auction Sale Catalogue* lists the following works by Coleridge: *The Friend*, 3 vols.; *Aids to Reflection; Church and State;* and *Confessions of an Enquiring Spirit*, 6 vols., foolscap 8vo, cloth (London, 1837–39); *Biographia Literaria: or my Literary Life and Opinions*, 2 vols., foolscap 8vo, cloth (London, 1847); *Literary Remains*, collected and edited by H. N. Coleridge, 4 vols., 8vo, cloth (London, 1836–38); *Dramatic Works and Poems*, edited by Derwent Coleridge, 2 vols., post 8vo, calf, gilt (London, 1852).

to ponder over Milton to get the meaning. Coleridge declares, "If this be called obscurity, let it be remembered that it is such an obscurity as is a compliment to the reader; not that vicious obscurity which proceeds from a muddled head."[51] Poetry may be pondered over at leisure but sermons must go straight to their mark, instantly intelligible.[52]

Clearness is a relative quality. It was thought of by Beecher in terms of reception by the audience. What might be clearness in poetry might be obscurity in public speaking. All through this discussion of style, as indeed, through the entire discussion of Beecher's rhetorical theory, there has run this thought of the economy of the auditor's attention. Beecher, as I have pointed out repeatedly, was not interested in the permanence of his work from a literary point of view. His genius did not run to essays or to novels but to sermons. He wrote some essays of fine quality and a novel of some merit, but these did not satisfy his soul's desire. He thought that preaching was nobler work. Of sermons that were more concerned with their literary quality than with creating nobler manhood, he declared, "People say, 'Those sermons are fit to be printed.' They are fit for nothing else. They are essays. They are sections of books."[53] Beecher knew that oral style militated against literary permanence, but he was content to let his sermons be

[51] Coleridge, *Lectures and Notes on Shakespeare and Other English Poets*, ed. T. Ashe (London: Bohn, 1883), p. 520: "The reader of Milton must always be on his duty; he is surrounded with sense; it rises in every line; every word is to the purpose. There are no lazy intervals; all has been considered, and demands and merits observation. If this be called obscurity, let it be remembered that it is such an obscurity as is a compliment to the reader; not that vicious obscurity which proceeds from a muddled head."

[52] Oliver Wendell Holmes has stressed the necessity of being instantly intelligible in lecturing. "A thoroughly popular lecture ought to have nothing in it which five hundred people cannot all take in a flash, just as it is uttered" (*The Autocrat of the Breakfast Table*, p. 139).

[53] *Yale Lectures* (1st ser.), p. 186.

printed as sermons. He tells us, "I have never read one of my sermons after it was printed that I did not burn to reconstruct and improve it. I have never attempted to rewrite one of them that I did not find it would lose in freedom and directness more than it gained in literary excellence."[54] Beecher's concept of style, and this is the point I am trying to make, was conditioned by its effect[55] upon the audience. He knew that the form of his sermons, from one point of view, was faulty, but results, not form, were his chief consideration.

D

Beecher's concern with persuasion appears in his formal statement of what style is. In the following paragraph he gives concepts of style that have been set forth by De Quincey, Buffon, and a description that would in some measure satisfy J. Middleton Murry's requirements for an adequate concept of style. Embodying the idea is not sufficient, nor is the revelation of the speaker's personality enough to portray Beecher's idea of style. For him, style must be effective expression; it must contemplate moving an audience to action.

Style is only the outside form which thoughts take on when embodied in language. Style, then, must conform to the nature of the man who employs it, as the saying goes, "Style is the man." In general, it may be said, that is the best style which is the least obtrusive, which lets through the truth most nearly in its absolute accuracy and purity. The truths of religion, in a simple and transparent style, shine as the sunlight on the fields and mountains, revealing all things in their proper forms and natural colors; but an artificial and gorgeous style, like a cathedral window, may let in some light, yet in blotches of purple and blue that spot the audience, and produce grotesqueness and unnatural effects.[56]

[54] *Preface to Sermons*, edited by Lyman Abbott (Harper & Bros., 1868).

[55] It is interesting that Poe gave this as the first consideration in his "*Philosophy of Composition*" (J. B. Moore, *Selections from Poe's Literary Criticism* [New York, 1926], p. 31).

[56] *Yale Lectures* (1st ser.), p. 228.

The three concepts of style expressed in this paragraph I shall take up in turn. First, "Style is only the outside form which thoughts take on when embodied in language." This definition of style is suggestive of De Quincey, who, in fact, employs the word *embody* in the same sense as does Beecher. In the following quotation, it will be noticed also that Wordsworth held to the same idea of style. De Quincey writes:

The more closely any exercise of mind is connected with what is internal and individual in the sensibilities—that is, with what is philosophically termed *subjective*—precisely in that degree, and the more subtly, does the style or the embodying of the thoughts cease to be a mere separable ornament, and in fact the more does the manner, as we expressed it before, become confluent with the matter. In saying this, we do but vary the form of what we once heard delivered on this subject by Mr. Wordsworth. His remark was by far the weightiest thing we ever heard on the subject of style; and it was this: that it is in the highest degree unphilosophic to call language or diction "the dress of thoughts." And what was it then that he would substitute? Why this: he would call it "the incarnation of thoughts." Never in one word was so profound a truth conveyed. Mr. Wordsworth was thinking, doubtless, of poetry like his own: viz. that which is eminently meditative.[57]

Such a concept of style may be satisfactory for meditative poems but not for sermons which are neither poems nor meditative discourses. Sermons are communicative. De Quincey's and Wordsworth's concept of style is inadequate to Beecher's understanding of the term. Nor does the next concept taken up fulfil the communicative requirement. Buffon in saying "Style is the man" evidently thought of the revelation of the individuality of the speaker or writer as the main thing.

The well written works are the only ones that will go down to posterity. The amount of knowledge in a book, the peculiarity of facts, the novelty of the discoveries are not sure warrants of immortality. If the works that contain these are concerned with minor objects; if they are written without taste, without nobility, without inspiration, they will perish; since

[57] *Essays on Style, Rhetoric, and Language*, edited by F. N. Scott, p. 118.

the knowledge, facts, and discoveries, being easily detached, are passed on to others, and even gain intrinsically when appropriated by more gifted hands, these things are external to the man; style is the man himself.[58]

But Beecher was not interested in the expression of the individuality of the speaker aside from its power to create response in the audience. He wanted to affect a body of hearers. He was not interested so much in the immortality of his sermons as he was in the immortality of the souls of his parishioners. The necessity laid upon style to bring about some change which the speaker desires seems to be the gist of Stendhal's definition to which J. Middleton Murry gives assent.

I do not think that anyone has ever more resolutely reduced the art of writing to essentials than Stendhal. He had an analytical and critical mind; there was some reason to expect that he would give the best of all definitions of style. He did so. Naturally, since Stendhal was the author, it reads like a definition. "Style is this: to add to a given thought all the circumstances fitted to produce the whole effect that the thought ought to produce."[59]

Stendhal's definition speaks of producing an effect. This concept parallels Beecher's in this respect. Beecher said, "An artificial and gorgeous style . . . . produces grotesqueness and unnatural effects." The implication is that a good style will produce the effects that the speaker strives for. Beecher's choice of words and phrases, and his use of sentences, were all determined by their ability to produce the effects that they ought to produce. Persuasion is the premise of Beecher's rhetorical theory.

Had Beecher been an exhaustive student of rhetoric, he might have constructed a theory of style upon his premise that ideas must be so expressed as to make them move an audience to action. And if he had, he might have approximated Aris-

[58] "Essay on Style," Lane Cooper's *Theories of Style* (New York, 1907), p. 178.

[59] J. Middleton Murry, *The Problem of Style* (Oxford University Press, 1922), p. 79.

totle's theory of style, for it, too, is predicated upon persuasion. When we realize that entire textbooks have been written upon the subject of style, Beecher's remarks seem incomplete. And although he barely touches upon the essentials of style, these essentials are such as to give us an idea of the sound practical sense that guided his efforts in speaking.

Inadequate as are Beecher's comments, it is apparent that he went right to the heart of the difference between the requirements of a style for spoken discourse and a style for written discourse. He insists that words and phrases be chosen that will sound well on the ear. Words and phrases must be chosen that will conserve the attention of the audience, thus emphasizing Herbert Spencer's principle of economy. Sentences suitable for literary expression may not be palpable enough for public speaking. His insight into the nature of sentences for oral style is as penetrating, if not as illuminating, as that of such a distinguished *littérateur* as De Quincey. Beecher's concept of style, phrased albeit not so competently as Stendhal's, contains much the same truth.

Beecher held no criterion of literary permanence before his eyes to obscure his ideal of preaching. The standards of composition for the written word are not the same as those for the spoken word, Beecher knew full well. Many rewards have to be forsworn by him who chooses to speak extempore, and no one was more aware of these penalties than Beecher. But if he suffered no illusions as to the disadvantages attendant on composing in the presence of an audience, he, likewise, was not blind to its advantages. What matter if grammar marred his sentences, what matter if his sentences followed no elaborate pattern, what matter if no one ever read his sermons,[60] he be-

---

[60] But the truth of the matter is that people did read his sermons, not only in the United States but in England. Mr. Pond relates: "In one room alone I found files of Mr. Clarke's publications running back as far as 1850; I took down the

lieved that he who preaches unwritten sermons is the true preacher, for only in such speaking can the preacher become *en rapport* with his audience.

---

first volume and saw on the first column of the first page, 'A sermon by the Rev. Henry Ward Beecher, preached in Plymouth Church, Brooklyn.' and reported especially for that periodical. I had a curiosity to see whether during Mr. Beecher's trouble the publications had been discontinued, so I went through every number up to 1886, and found that not in one *number* had there been such a hiatus. For twenty-five years, through tempest and sunshine and darkness and light, Mr. James Clarke had published every week one of Mr. Beecher's sermons" (J. B. Pond, *A Summer in England with Henry Ward Beecher* [New York, 1887], p. 97).

There are ten volumes of *Plymouth Pulpit Sermons* averaging 600 pages in length. In 1868, Lyman Abbott brought out a de luxe edition of Beecher's sermons in two volumes which total 970 pages. His *Life Thoughts* (1858), sold 25,000 copies the first year of its publication. His *Lectures to Young Men* (1845), is still in print. In the public library at Battle Creek, Michigan, I found that the volume of sermons *Evolution and Religion* (1885) had been withdrawn in 1930; evidence that he is still read.

CONCLUSION

A

Aristotle's *Rhetoric*, Richard Jebb declared, is, without doubt, the driest book that has ever been written. Such an epithet cannot properly be applied to Beecher's lectures that deal with the composition of the sermon. In their readableness Beecher's lectures may be compared to Cicero's *De oratore*. To be sure, Beecher did not compose such a treatise as *De oratore*, but for the sake of understanding their nature the comparison is useful. Both Cicero and Beecher speak out of the fulness of their experience. Both begin their remarks on their art by stating that they desire merely to drop some helpful, practical suggestions gathered from their own experience as orators.

Like Cicero, Beecher did not profess to set forth a system of rhetoric. He explicitly denied any intention of elaborating a rhetorical theory. He did not attempt to tell how a sermon ought to be prepared, but how he actually composed his sermons. His remarks are intensely personal, and due allowances, therefore, have to be made. For as Coleridge has said, "Experience is like the stern light of a ship at sea; it enlightens only the track which has been passed over." Beecher could not detach himself from preaching long enough to view his art critically in all its aspects. Preaching, not teaching, was for him the immutable necessity. His lectures that touch upon the problems of preaching were not painstakingly prepared in the study and delivered word for word from manuscript. Such a procedure would have been foreign, if not repugnant, to Beecher's nature and training.

Beecher's usual practice of speaking extempore was followed in his lectures on preaching, and for this reason they bear all the attendant strengths and weaknesses of such a practice. Their chief strength was in their interestingness and suggestiveness. His listeners wanted him to talk engagingly out of his experience. This he did to their complete satisfaction, if not to the strict demands of a system of rhetoric. He spoke in broad outlines and let the audience fill in the details from their experience and study. The lectures illustrate what they attempt to teach—how to win and hold the attention of an audience. Their chief weakness was in their lack of thoroughness. Extempore speaking does not permit exhaustive treatment. Had Beecher carefully set forth a system of rhetoric, posterity might have acclaimed him as a rhetorician, but his immediate hearers would have labeled him a pedant.

Although it is difficult to piece whatever fragments of a rhetorical nature found in his lectures into a coherent scheme of thought and call it Beecher's rhetorical theory; and, although his reflections on rhetoric have but minor scientific value; yet, his observations have value for the student of rhetoric in that they illustrate an artist attempting to explain how he subjugated his material to his purpose.

B

In evaluating Beecher's rhetorical theory I have concluded that he added to our knowledge of the instruments of persuasion in two directions. In the matter of sermon organization for extempore speaking, he stated that the common people, gathered together in large numbers, are most effectively persuaded by a line of facts or a series of parables. As I have pointed out, the parts of these formulas have been recognized to be effective in isolation, but before Beecher's time, or since, no one showed that an entire discourse could be built upon these structures. Speakers, like Conwell, Talmage, and Spurgeon, have employed them without inquiring into the theory involved. Empirically, speakers have utilized this organization for extempore speaking; Beecher rationalized it.

The other addition to our understanding of the instruments of persuasion is in the matter of illustrations. The dominant characteristic of Beecher's preaching was its profuse employment of illustrations, the instrument which suited perfectly Beecher's extempore speaking. Illustrations constituted small units, like squads in a platoon, that could easily be manipulated. Variety, a cornerstone of Beecher's rhetorical theory and practice, could be introduced through the illustration. Beecher enumerated eleven uses of the illustration—the most complete analysis of the illustration that has ever been made as far as I have been able to discover. Three uses of the illustration appear as original deductions by Beecher: (1) the illustration may provide for a variety of hearers; (2) the illustration helps the speaker to say indirectly what would be inexpedient to say directly; and (3) the illustration conserves the attention of the audience. Beecher's thorough examination of the illustration is the one exception to the general character of his remarks.

C

In stating that illustrations aid the speaker in saying indirectly what he deems unsuitable to say directly, Beecher indicates that he thought of rhetoric as "the art of appearance," to use Aristotle's phrase, or as the art of finding the "principles of success," to use the phrase of George Henry Lewes. This emphasis on success does not imply deception but expediency. It will be recalled that Aristotle said, "The whole discipline of rhetoric aims at appearance."[1] After Beecher had given an illustration of what he meant by this use of the illustration, he said, "You may say that was not the most honorable way, and that it was a weakness. It may have been so; but I conquered them by that very weakness."[2] Beecher's remark is not unlike Aristotle's statement, "Owing to the infirmities of the hearer style can do much."[3]

It is unthinkable that Beecher, as a student at Amherst, with his intense interest in rhetoric, almost to the exclusion of his other studies, would have left unstudied Aristotle's *Rhetoric*. It is true that the *Rhetoric* does not appear in the list of books in Beecher's library, but neither does the *Auction Sales Catalogue* contain the titles of Whately, Blair, and Campbell on rhetoric. These treatises on rhetoric were required textbooks

[1] *Rhetoric* 1404a.

[2] *Yale Lectures* (1st ser.), p. 167; other examples of the emphasis upon rhetoric as the art of finding the principles of success are seen in the following. Beecher was asked, "If you went into a neighborhood where Universalism or Spiritualism prevailed, would you preach against them, or pass them by?" Beecher replied, "I cannot answer that question precisely, it would depend on so many considerations; the first of which might be how far the preacher was infected with it. Secondly, what class of the community was infected. If the thinking class, and the influential, three or four families, I might take one course; but if it was only the ignorant and those that had no influence upon society, I might take another course" (*Yale Lectures* [1st ser.], p. 23). At another time Beecher was asked, "Suppose a man tries to work himself up to a feeling of enthusiasm by action and increased emphasis, can he be successful?" Beecher replied, "In addressing a congregation a man may use the language of a feeling for the sake of getting and propagating the feeling. Indeed, when it comes to preaching, I think it would be a great deal better to act as though you had the feeling, even if you had not, for its effect in carrying your audience whither you wish to carry them" (*Yale Lectures* [1st ser.], p. 126).

[3] *Rhetoric* 1404a.

and were probably disposed of on the completion of his college career at the public auction which was then customary. Be that as it may, Beecher learned of Aristotle's principles indirectly through his study of Whately, not to mention the others. The first edition of Whately's *Elements of Rhetoric* appeared in 1829; Beecher entered Amherst College in 1830. Students would turn with zeal to a new textbook. In the Introduction to his work, Whately gives a review of rhetorical thought down through the centuries, and says the following of Aristotle, "Among the ancients, Aristotle, the earliest whose works are extant, may safely be pronounced to be also the best of the systematic writers of rhetoric."

One is able to deduce from the fact that Beecher looked upon the illustration as an instrument of persuasion that he thought of rhetoric, as did Aristotle, not as the art of persuasion but as the faculty of finding all the available means of persuasion in a given case. Similarly, Beecher is Aristotelian in approaching the problems of invention, arrangement, and style, from the point of view of the audience in order to persuade them. For Beecher, as for Aristotle, there had to be perfect adjustment of the means of persuasion to the needs of the audience. It is fundamental that the speaker know human nature in order that he may adapt his discourse to its needs. Aristotle in Book II of the *Rhetoric* goes into detail about human nature; here Beecher is content to exhort his listeners to know the motives that control human behavior. Another similarity to Aristotle's *Rhetoric* is found in Beecher's belief that rhetoric deals with questions involving probability. Matters of scientific fact do not admit the employment of the instruments of persuasion. Fundamentally, Beecher's theory of rhetoric is Aristotelian.

D

A most important influence upon Beecher's rhetorical theory and practice of rhetoric was a thoroughgoing belief in Herbert

Spencer's "principle of economy." Beecher stated that Herbert Spencer's essay on style was the best with which he was familiar. Beecher believed, accordingly, that the speaker should employ those instruments that would aid in flashing the meaning upon the audience. The audience should not be required to dig for the meaning. Beecher was sensitive to the relative nature of the quality of clearness; for oral discourse it was one thing, for written composition another. Beecher's use of the illustration to rest the attention of the audience is an original application of the principle of economy. His advocacy of the use of Anglo-Saxon words is identical with Spencer's application of the principle.

E

In preferring to address his appeals to the common people, Beecher was in harmony with the political and social thought of the nineteenth century. Beecher loved the common people. In early nineteenth-century English literature, the same confidence in the common people was evinced by, to mention no others, Crabbe and Wordsworth. Faith in the common people was the great theme of Walt Whitman's writing and lecturing. While choosing to learn of life first-hand, Beecher did not ignore the services of books. He was a wide reader. In his choice library of fifteen thousand books, every field of human interest was represented. Books dealing with the physical and social sciences were especially numerous. Beecher, in a sense, acted as an interpreter of the world of science to the lay mind. He early saw the significance of the theory of evolution and its bearing on Christianity. His first-hand observations of nature were checked in his library with those of reputed scientists. His love of nature was paralleled by his love of art. His aesthetic taste was responsible for the placing of many valuable works of art in his library and home. In every conceivable corner of human interest, Beecher searched for materials with which to stock his mind.

Beecher's exposition of his own creative process, aside from evincing a close scrutiny of his mental habits, is not unusual. Other public speakers have employed similar processes of preparation and execution. His practice of composing in the presence of his audience not only best suited his creative temperament but permitted the nicest possible adjustment to the ever changing needs of his congregation. Beecher's entire life was a general preparation. During the week preceding a sermon, he brooded over several possible themes. On Sunday morning he went into his study, chose the theme that was ripest, and outlined it. Then, going into the pulpit, he preached upon the chosen theme. On occasions he abandoned his prepared theme in favor of another that seemed to promise a closer adaptation to the needs of his audience.

In his preaching, pathetic proof was emphasized more than logical proof. He assumed that people feel more than they think, especially people gathered together in large congregations. He recognized that the press had usurped very largely the educational function of the pulpit, which was once one of its primary duties. He felt that it was his duty to spiritualize knowledge, to show that a unity ran through everything. In a word, to employ De Quincey's useful distinction, Beecher emphasized the literature of power rather than the literature of knowledge. Beecher, it should be pointed out, however, always utilized the literature of power to effect a noble purpose. On the other hand, he was thoroughly capable of employing logical proof when occasion demanded it, as is shown by the "Liverpool Address," but usually his aim demanded other forms.

I have already referred to Beecher's contribution to our understanding of the use of planning for extempore speaking. With Beecher, form and idea were simultaneously born. To be effective in extempore speaking, the orator should not hold himself too rigidly to his preconceived plan, especially if that plan should fail to hold attention. The criterion of symmetry as applied to literature should not be applied to extempore speeches. Nor should the criterion of literary permanency be applied to them. Speeches must be judged by other standards. Their immediate effect upon the audience is of first importance.

In the matter of style, Beecher's remarks are based upon the necessity of communication. A speech requires participation not contemplation on the part of the audience. The structural elements of style and the qualities of style mentioned by Beecher are unimportant except that they give evidence of his acquaintance with the rhetorical treatises of others on style, and indicate an understanding of the differences in the requirements of style in written and spoken discourse, a matter to which I have already called attention. In his advocacy of the use of language of everyday speech, Beecher is a forerunner of the present-day tendency in the teaching of composition to discard the stiff, formal, bookish words. I presume that Beecher knew of De Quincey's essays on rhetoric and language. The *Auction Sale Catalogue*, as I have indicated, lists De Quincey's works. Beecher's analysis of the difference in sentence structure for written discourse and public address is interestingly similar to De Quincey's analysis of the differences in the sentence structure of Burke and Dr. Johnson, which is due, De Quincey thinks, in some measure, to the demands of extempore speaking. Beecher's use of the word *embodiment*, in speaking of the various concepts of style, is the same as De Quincey's use of the word. The concept of style which is satisfactory to Beecher concurs, as regards the necessity of communication, with Stendhal's definition of style as put forward by J. Middleton Murry.

May I repeat that one will not find in the remarks of

Beecher relative to the thought and language aspects of preaching a complete or satisfactory system of rhetoric. His remarks would not make an acceptable textbook, although they surely would make stimulating collateral reading for a course in public speaking. In truth, Beecher did not design to write a rhetoric that would compare with Whately's *Elements of Rhetoric*. Beecher occupied a lectureship that was founded to give him the opportunity of talking out of his own successful experience. He was supposed to divulge his secrets of how to succeed in the pulpit. This is quite different from occupying a chair of rhetoric as did Whately, Blair, and Newman. Beecher attempted to point out what instruments of persuasion were, according to his own experience, most effective in extempore speaking. Just as De Quincey had pondered over the effect of publication upon rhetorical theory, Beecher pondered over the effect upon rhetorical theory of composing in the presence of an audience with a view to their persuasion. One wonders whether if Beecher had seriously undertaken and completed such a task in the quiet of his study it would not have been a contribution to rhetorical theory of first importance. But in a larger sense, it is not to be regretted that Beecher did not develop in greater detail his theory of rhetoric. If he had been more of a rhetorician he might have been less of a preacher. Over-anxiety for form leads to decadence of the creative imagination. Walt Whitman well said "Who troubles himself about his ornaments or fluency is lost."

APPENDIX I

CHRONOLOGY

June 24, 1813	Born in Litchfield, Connecticut
1830	Entered Amherst College
1834	Graduated from Amherst College
1837	Graduated from Lane Theological Seminary
1838	Ordained at Presbyterian Church, Lawrenceburg, Indiana
1839	Installed at Second Presbyterian Church, Indianapolis, Indiana
1847	Installed at Plymouth Church, Brooklyn, New York
1850	Editorial, "Shall We Compromise?"
1850	First journey to England and Europe
1856	Supports Fremont for presidency
1856	Ransoms Negro girls in Plymouth pulpit
1859	Invites Lincoln to speak in Plymouth Church
1861–63	Editor of *Independent*
1863	Delivers series of anti-slavery speeches in England
April 14, 1865	Delivers address at raising of flag at Fort Sumter
1855–78	Trustee of Amherst College
1870–80	Editor of *Christian Union*
1870	Publishes first volume of *Life of Christ*
1870	Gives lecture on "Successful Preaching"
1872	First of *Yale Lectures on Preaching*
1873	Second of *Yale Lectures on Preaching*
1874	Third of *Yale Lectures on Preaching*
1876	Lecture on Oratory, Philadelphia
1878–87	Chaplain of the thirteenth New York regiment
1884	Supported Grover Cleveland for presidency
1886	Tour of England
1886	Delivers lectures on "Address to Students" and "True Preaching"
March 8, 1887	Died in Brooklyn, New York.

APPENDIX II

PUBLISHED WORKS OF BEECHER

1844 *Twelve Lectures to Young Men*
1855 First *Star Papers*
1855 *Life Thoughts*
1859 More *Star Papers*
1862 *Royal Truths*
1862 *Eyes and Ears*
1863 *Freedom and War*
1864 *American Rebellion*
1865 *Sermon Briefs*
1867 *Norwood*
1867 *Dramatization of Norwood*
1868 *Prayers from Plymouth Pulpit;* also, 1886, 1892, 1895
1868 Two volumes of sermons, de luxe edition
1870 *The Overture of Angels*
1870 *Lecture-Room Talks*
1870 *Life of Christ*
1872 *Yale Lectures on Preaching* (1st ser.)
1873 *Yale Lectures on Preaching* (2d ser.)
1874 *Yale Lectures on Preaching* (3d ser.)
1874 *Pleasant Talks about Fruits, Flowers and Farming*
1875 *A Summer Parish*
1876 *Lecture on Oratory*
1884 Two letters on the reconstruction of the Southern States
1885 *Evolution and Religion* (one of ten volumes of sermons)
1885 *Comforting Thoughts*
1886 *A Summer in England with Henry Ward Beecher*
1887 *Beecher as a Humorist*
1887 *Corning Memorial*
1887 *Beecher Memorial* (Knight) also (Bok, ed.)
1887 *Patriotic Addresses*
1890 *The Crown of Life*
1893 *Bible Studies*
1895 *Metaphors and Similes*
1904 *Treasury of Illustrations*
1913 *Lectures and Orations* (Newell Dwight Hillis, ed.)

APPENDIX III

BRIEF OF THE "LIVERPOOL ADDRESS"[1]

I. Introduction
   A. For more than twenty-five years I have been made perfectly familiar with popular assemblies in all parts of my country except in the South.
      1. There has not for the whole of that time been a single day when it would have been safe for me to go south of the Mason's and Dixon's line in my own country, and all for one reason: my solemn, earnest, persistent testimony against that which I consider to be the most atrocious thing under the sun—the system of American slavery in a great free republic.
   B. Since I have been in England, although I have met with greater kindness and courtesy on the part of most than I deserved, yet on the other hand, I perceive that the Southern influence prevails to some extent in England.
      1. I understand it perfectly and I have always held it to be an unfailing truth that where a man had a cause that would bear examination he was perfectly willing to have it spoken about.
      2. It is a matter of very little consequence to me whether I speak here tonight or not. But, one thing is certain—if you do permit me to speak here tonight you will hear very plain talking.
         a) And if I do not mistake the tone and the temper of Englishmen, they had rather have a man who opposes them in a manly way than a sneak that agrees with them in an unmanly way.
         b) If I can carry you with me by sound convictions I shall be immensely glad; but if I cannot carry you with me by

---

[1] This brief indicates that when occasion demanded Beecher could and did employ logical proof. Cf. E. H. Henrickson, *Elements of Persuasion in Henry Ward Beecher's Speeches in England in 1863*, M.A. Thesis, University of Iowa, 1929.

facts and sound arguments, I do not wish you to go with me at all; and all I ask is fair play.

II. Discussion

  A. There are two dominant races in history: the Germanic and the Romanic.

    1. The Germanic races tend to personal liberty, to a sturdy individualism, to civil and to political liberty.

    2. The Romanic race tends to absolutism in government, it is clannish; it loves chieftains; it develops a people that crave strong and showy governments to support and plan for them.

    3. The Anglo-Saxon race belongs to the great German family.

      a) The Anglo-Saxon carries self-government and self-development with him wherever he goes.

      b) He has popular Government and popular Industry

        (1) The power to create riches is just as much a part of the Anglo-Saxon virtues as the power to create good order and social safety.

        (2) The things required for prosperous labor, prosperous manufactures, and prosperous commerce are three:

          (*a*) First, liberty; second, liberty; third, liberty.

  B. First there must be liberty to follow those laws of business which experience has developed, without imposts or restrictions, or governmental intrusions.

  C. There must be liberty to distribute and exchange products of industry in any market without burdensome tariffs, without imposts, and without vexatious regulations.

  D. The third is the necessity of an intelligent and free race of customers.

    1. It is a necessity of every manufacturing and commercial people that their customers should be very wealthy and intelligent.

      a) To whom do the tradesmen of Liverpool sell the most goods at the highest profit?

        (1) The poor man buys simply for his body

        (2) A man well off buys for the satisfaction of sentiment and taste, as well as of sense

      b) The whole laboring community is as much interested and profited as the mere merchant, in this buying and selling of the higher grades, in the greater varieties and quantities.

    (1) The law of price is the skill

    (2) Genius carries the whole market and gets the highest price.

2. That nation is the best customer that is freest, because freedom works prosperity, industry, and wealth.

  a) Great Britain, then, aside from moral considerations, has a direct commercial and pecuniary interest in the liberty, civilization, and wealth of every people and every nation on the globe.

  b) Now, Great Britain's chief want is what? They have said your chief want is cotton. I deny it. Your chief want is consumers.

  c) The doctrine how to make customers is a great deal more important to Great Britain than the doctrine How to raise cotton

3. There are no more continents to be discovered.

  a) If you are to have a better market there must be some kind of process invented to make the old fields better.

  b) You must civilize the world in order to make a better class of purchasers.

    (1) If you were to press Italy down again under the feet of despotism, Italy, discouraged, could draw but very few supplies from you.

    (2) If Hungary asks to be unshackled as a nation—if by freedom she will rise in virtue and intelligence, then by freedom she will acquire a more multifarious industry, which she will be willing to exchange for manufacturing.

    (3) Every nation that rises from barbarism to industry becomes a better customer.

(Interruption)

4. What will be the result if this present struggle shall eventuate in the separation of America, and making the South a slave territory, and the North a free territory? What will be the first result?

  a) It would be an empire of twelve millions of people.

    (1) Eight millions are black and four millions white.

    (2) Consider that two-thirds are miserably poor, unbuying blacks.

(3) You sagacious Britons are busy in favoring the establishment of an empire from ocean to ocean that should have fewest customers and the largest non-buying population.

b) Notice the difference between free labor and slave-labor to produce cultivated land.

(1) Virginia has only 15,000 more square miles of land than the state of New York but Virginia has only 15,000 square miles improved, while New York has 20,000 square miles improved. Of unimproved land Virginia has about 23,000 square miles, and New York only about 10,000 square miles.

(2) Maryland has 2,000 more square miles of land than Massachusetts; but Maryland has about 4,000 square miles of land improved, Massachusetts has 3,200 square miles. Maryland has 2,800 unimproved square miles of land, while Massachusetts has but 1,800 square miles unimproved.

(3) The state of Georgia has 12,000 more square miles of land than Pennsylvania. Georgia has only about 9,800 square miles of improved land, Pennsylvania 2,300,000 acres more than Georgia. Georgia has about 25,600 square miles of unimproved land, and Pennsylvania has only 10,400 square miles, or about 10,-000,000 acres less of unimproved land than Georgia.

c) What can England make for the poor white population of such a future empire, and for her slave population?

(1) What carpets, what linens, what cottons can you sell them? What machines, what looking-glasses, what combs, what leather, what books, what pictures, what engravings?

(2) (Refutation) You may sell ships to a few, but what ships can you sell to two-thirds of the populations of poor whites and blacks?

(3) This very day, in the Slave States of America there are eight millions out of twelve millions that are not, and cannot be your customers from the very laws of trade.

5. (Refutation) There are some apparent drawbacks that may suggest themselves. The first is that the interests of England

consist in drawing from any country its raw material. There is
an interest but it is not now the chief interest of England.

a) England does not want merely to pay prices for that which
   brute labor produces, but to get a price for that which
   brain labor produces.

b) Your interest lies beyond all peradventure in customers.

6. Now it is said that if the South should be allowed to be sepa-
rate there will be no tariff; and England can trade with her;
but, if the South remains in the United States it will be bound
by a tariff, and English goods will be excluded from it.

a) Let me tell you that the first tariff ever proposed in America was not only supported by Southerners, but was origi-
   nated by the peculiar structure of Southern society.

   (1) They proposed that taxes and representation should
       be the basis of five black men counting as three white
       men. In a short time it was found impossible to raise
       these taxes in the South, and then they cast about for
       a better way, and the tariff scheme was proposed.

   (2) The tariff had its origin in Southern weaknesses and
       necessities, and not in the Northern cities.

b) New England accepted it, and saying "It is the law of the
   land," conformed her industry to it; and when she got her
   capital embarked in mills and machinery she grew in favor
   of it.

c) The South, beginning to feel, as she grew stronger, that
   it was against her interest to continue the system, sought
   to have the tariff modified, and brought it down; though
   Henry Clay, a Southern man, himself, was the immortal
   champion of the tariff.

d) I have lived to see the time when, just before the war broke
   out, it might be said that the thinking men of America
   were ready for free-trade.

e) It was the South that obliged the North to put the Morrill
   tariff on.

f) There is nothing more certain in the future than that
   America is bound to join Great Britain in the world wide
   doctrine of free trade.

(Conclusion) Here, then, so far as this argument is concerned I rest my
             case, saying that it seems to me that in an argument ad-

dressed to a commercial people it was perfectly fair to represent that their commercial and manufacturing interests tallied with their moral sentiments; and as by birth, by blood, by history, by moral feeling, and by everything Great Britain is connected with the liberty of the world, God has joined interest and conscience, head and heart; so that you ought to be in favor of liberty everywhere. There I have got quite a speech out already, if I do not get any more. *Patriotic Addresses*, p. 529.

E. It is said that the South is fighting for just that independence of which I have been speaking.
　1. But the South is divided on that subject.
　2. They went out of the Union because slave-property is not recognized in it.
　　a) There are two ways of reaching the slave-property in the Union; the one by exerting the direct Federal authority; but they could not do that, they conceived it to be forbidden. The second was by indirect influence.
　　b) By limiting slave territory you lay the foundation for the final extinction of slavery.
　　　(1) Slavery poisons the land on which it grows.
　　　(2) I do not stand on my own testimony alone.
　3. By the constitution of Montgomery they legalized slavery, and they made it the organic law of the land.
　　a) The very Constitution which they said they could not live under when they left the Union they took again immediately afterwards, altering it in only one point, and that was, making the fundamental law of the land to be slavery.
　　b) Let no man say that slavery had nothing to do with the Secession.

F. (Refutation) But I know that you say, you cannot help sympathizing with a gallant people.

G. (Refutation) It is said that the North is fighting for Union and not for emancipation.
　1. The North is fighting for Union for that *insures* emancipation.
　2. We are fighting for the Union, because we believe that preamble which explains the very reason for which the Union was constituted.

H. (Refutation) Well, next it is said, that the North treats the negro race worse than the South.

    1. For a period of twenty-five years the North went to sleep and permitted herself to be drugged and poisoned with the Southern prejudice against the black men.

    2. The colored man has been the football between the two parties in the North, and has suffered accordingly.

        a) Those men who undertook to stand up for the rights of all men—black as well as white—have increased in number; and now what party in the North represents those men that resist the evil prejudices of past years? The Republicans are that party.

        b) And who are those men in the North who have oppressed the negro? They are the Peace Democrats; and the prejudice for which in England you are attempting to punish me, is a prejudice raised by the men who have opposed me all my life.

I. (Refutation) I am going to read you some questions that were sent after me from Glasgow, purporting to be from a working man.

    1. And first the bill for emancipation in Missouri, to which this money was denied, was a bill which was drawn by what we call "Log-rollers," who inserted in it an enormously disproportionate price for slaves.

    2. Now as to those States that had passed "black" laws, as we call them, they are filled with Southern immigrants, and it was their votes, or the Northern states pandering for political reasons to theirs, that passed in those States the infamous "black" laws.

    3. Now as to the state of New York, it is asked whether a negro is not obliged to have a certain freehold property, or a certain amount of property before he can vote. It is so still in North Carolina and Rhode Island for *white* folks—it is so in New York state.

    4. Is it not a fact that in most of the Northern States laws exist precluding negroes from equal civil and political rights with the whites? Let us compare the condition of the negro in the North and the South, and that will tell the story.

        a) By express law the South takes away from the slave all

attributes of manhood, and calls him "chattel," which is another word for "cattle."

b) The South denies the right of legal permanent marriage to the slave.

c) There is not a state, county, or town, or school district in the North, where, if any man dare to violate the family of the poorest black man, there would not be an indignation that would overwhelm him.

d) In the South by statutory law it is a penitentiary offence to teach the black men to read and write. In the North not only are hundreds and thousands of dollars of state money expended in teaching colored people, but they have their own schools, their own academies, their own churches, their own ministers, their own lawyers.

e) In the South, black men are bred, exactly as cattle are bred in the North, for the market and for sale.

f) In the South the slave can own nothing by law but in the single city of New York there are ten million dollars of money belonging to the free colored people.

g) In the South no colored man can determine where he will work, nor at what he will work. But in the North—except in the great cities, where we are crowded by foreigners— in any country part, the black man may choose his trade and work at it, and is just as much protected by the laws as any white man in the land.

h) And now, for the first time in the history of America a colored man has received a commission under the broad seal and signature of the President of the United States.

J. There is another fact that I wish to allude to—not for the sake of reproach or blame, but by way of claiming your more lenient consideration—and that is, that slavery was entailed upon us by your action.

1. Against the earnest protests of the colonists the then Government of Great Britain—I will concede, not knowing what were the mischiefs—ignorantly, but in point of fact, forced slave traffic on the unwilling colonies.

2. Suppose a child is born with hereditary disease; suppose this disease was entailed upon him by parents who had contracted it by their own misconduct, would it be fair that those par-

ents, that had brought into the world the diseased child, should rail at that child because it was diseased?

K. I am every day asked when this war will end. I wish I could tell you but remember, slavery is the cause of the war.

    1. This war won't end until the cancer of slavery is cut out by the roots.

    2. President Lincoln said, "Tell your anti-slavery friends that I am coming out all right!"

III. Conclusion

A. I do not say that you ought not to be in the most friendly alliance with France or with Germany; but I do say that your own children, the off-spring of England, ought to be nearer to you than any people of strange tongue.

    1. If there have been any feelings of bitterness in America let me tell you they have been excited, rightly or wrongly, under the impression that Great Britain was going to intervene between us and our own lawful struggle.

    2. We accept it as a fact, and we say that the utterance of Lord Russell at Blairgowrie together with the declaration of the government in stopping war-steamers here has gone far toward quieting every fear and removing every apprehension from our minds.

B. (Refutation) I declare that, at no time for the ten years past—without any rule passed by the trustees, and without even a request from me—no decent man or woman has ever found molestation or trouble in walking into my church and sitting where he or she pleased.

C. (Refutation) The thinking men and the influential men of both parties are becoming more and more in favor of free-trade.

D. I say still further, that in all New England there is not a railway where a colored man cannot ride as freely as a white man.

APPENDIX IV

THE SCOPE OF MR. BEECHER'S PREACHING

The following list of Mr. Beecher's texts and themes for two years indicate one element of his pulpit power, namely, his variety, and interpret and partly illustrate his advice to the Yale Theological Students, "Never preach two sermons alike if you can help it" (cf. *supra.*, p. 75).

1. Thoughts of Death.—John 9:4
2. Peaceful Living.—Rom. 12:18
3. The Law of Liberty.—Gal. 5:1, 18
4. What is the Profit of Godliness.—I Tim. 4:18
5. The Religious Uses of Music.—Eph. 5:19
6. The Past and the Future.—Phil. 3:12-15
7. As to the Lord.—Col. 3:22, 23, 24.
8. Faithfulness to Conviction the Basis of Right Action.—Rom. 14:5
9. Earning a Livelihood.—Eph. 4:28
10. Soul Sight.—John 20:29
11. Moral Honesty and Moral Earnestness.—Luke 14:26, 27; John 14:6
12. The Use of Ideals.—I Cor. 1:28-31
13. Exterior and Interior Divine Providence.—Phil. 2:13
14. Motives of Action.—I Cor. 10:31
15. True Christian Toleration.—Acts 21:17-26
16. The Nature and Power of Humility.—Phil. 3:1
17. The Altars of Childhood Rebuilt.—I Kings 18:17
18. Through Fear to Love.—I John 3:2
19. Immortality.—I Cor. 15:19
20. Possibilities of the Future.—I John 3:2
21. Children.—Matt. 18:10
22. The Sense of the Ever-Present God.—Heb. 11:27
23. The Nature and Sources of Temptation.—James 1:13-14
24. The Temporal Advantages of Religion.—I Tim. 4:18
25. The Mercifulness of the Bible.—Ps. 119:64
26. The Life Completed in the Life That Is To Come.—Heb. 13:14
27. The Nature, Importance, and Liberties of Belief.—John 9:25-38
28. Healing Virtue in Christ.—Mark 5:24-34
29. The Christian Use of the Tongue.—Col. 3:17

30. Heroism.—Mark 12:41–44 and 14:3–9
31. The Atoning God.—Heb. 4:14–16
32. The New Testament Theory of Evolution.—I John 3:2, 3
33. Fact and Fancy.—II Cor. 4:18
34. All-Sidedness in Christian Life.—Eph. 6:13
35. Prayer.—I Tim. 2:1, 2
36. Cuba and the Brotherhood of Nations.—Gal. 3:28
37. Working and Waiting.—Eph. 6:13
38. The Moral Teaching of Suffering.—Rom. 5:6–8
39. The Nature of Christ.—Heb. 2:17, 18, and Heb. 4:16
40. The Science of Right Living.—Eph. 4:31, 32
41. Religious Constancy.—Heb. 6:3, 4
42. The Riches of God.—Eph. 2:4–7
43. Soul Power.—I Cor. 12:3
44. St. Paul's Creed.—Phil. 4:18
45. The Departed Christ.—John 16:7
46. The Naturalness of Faith.—II Cor. 5:7
47. Spiritual Manhood.—II Cor. 12:10
48. Special Providence.—Matt. 6:30
49. Keeping the Faith.—Heb. 3:6, 14, and Heb. 10:36
50. Charles Sumner.—Isa. 1:36
51. Saved by Hope.—Rom. 8:24, 25
52. Following Christ.—Matt. 4:17–22
53. The Primacy of Love.—I Cor. 1:18–24
54. Summer in the Soul.—Luke 17:21
55. Hindering Christianity.—Gal. 5:22–26
56. Soul-Relationship.—Gal. 3:26–29, and Eph. 11:19–22
57. Christian Joyfulness.—Rom. 12:12
58. The Secret of the Cross.—I Cor. 2:1–5
59. God's Grace.—Eph. 2:8
60. The Problem of Life.—I John 3:2, 3, and Rom. 8:18–21
61. Unjust Judgments.—Matt. 7:1
62. The Immortality of Good Work.—Rev. 14:13
63. The Delight of Self-sacrifice.—Matt. 20:28, and Phil. 2:1–11
64. Truth Speaking.—Eph. 4:25
65. Saved by Grace.—Eph. 2:18
66. The World's Growth.—I Cor. 4:20
67. Foundation Work.—Rom. 15:20
68. True Righteousness.—Phil. 3:9
69. The Work of Patience.—James 1:3, 4

APPENDIX V

BIBLIOGRAPHY

SOURCES CITED

ABBOTT, LYMAN (ed.). *Hints for Home Reading; Plans for Reading; Henry Ward Beecher.* New York: G. P. Putnam's Sons, 1880.

————. *Life of Henry Ward Beecher.* New York: Houghton, Mifflin Co., 1903.

ABBOTT, LYMAN, AND HALLIDAY, S. B. *Life of Henry Ward Beecher: A Sketch of His Career.* Hartford, Conn.: American Publishing Co., 1888.

American Humor. New York: G. P. Putnam's Sons, 1907.

Amherst College Catalogues for 1830–31; 1831–32; 1832–33; 1833–34.

Atlantic Monthly, Vol. XIII. January, 1864.

ARISTOTLE. *Rhetoric,* translation by R. C. Jebb. Cambridge University Press, 1909.

BAIN, ALEXANDER. *English Composition and Rhetoric.* London: Longmans Green, 1893.

BALDWIN, C. S. *College Manual of Rhetoric.* New York: Longmans Green & Co., 1903.

Baptist, The, December 20, 1930.

BARROWS, J. H. *Henry Ward Beecher, The Shakespeare of the Pulpit.* New York: Funk and Wagnalls, 1887.

BARRUS, CLARA. *Whitman and Burroughs, Comrades.* New York: Houghton, Mifflin Co., 1931.

BASCOM, JOHN. *Philosophy of Rhetoric.* Boston: Crosby and Ainsworth, 1866.

BAUTAIN, M. *The Art of Extempore Speaking.* New York: Charles Scribner, 1859.

Beecher, Henry Ward: As a Humorist. New York, 1894.

Beecher, Henry Ward: As His Friends Saw Him. Boston, 1904.

Beecher, Henry Ward: Crown of Life, ed. Mary Storr Haynes. New York, 1890.

BEECHER, HENRY WARD. *Eyes and Ears.* Boston, 1862.

————. *Lecture on Oratory.* Philadelphia, 1876.

————. *Lecture-Room Talks.* New York, 1870.

———. *Life of Christ*, Vol. I. New York, 1870.

———. *Metaphors and Similes*. New York, 1895.

———. *Norwood*. New York, 1867.

———. *New Star Papers*. New York, 1855.

———. *New Star Papers*. 1859.

———. *Orations and Addresses*, ed. N. D. Hillis. 1913.

———. *Life Thoughts*. New York, 1858.

———. *Patriotic Addresses*, ed. J. R. Howard. New York, 1887.

———. *Pleasant Talks about Fruits and Farming*. New York, 1874.

———. *Plymouth Pulpit Sermons* (de luxe edition), ed. Lyman Abbott. 1868.

———. *Plymouth Pulpit Sermons*, 10 volumes.

———. *Sermon Briefs*. Boston, 1904.

———. *Seven Lectures to Young Men*. Indianapolis, 1845.

———. *Summer in England with Henry Ward Beecher*. New York, 1886.

———. *Yale Lectures on Preaching* (1st, 2d, and 3d ser.). 1872, 1873, and 1874.

BEECHER, MRS. HENRY WARD. "Mr. Beecher as I Knew Him." *Ladies' Home Journal*. New York, 1891–92.

BEECHER, W. C., AND SCOVILLE, S., AND BEECHER, MRS. HENRY WARD. *Life and Letters of Henry Ward Beecher*. New York, 1888.

BLAIR, HUGH. *Lectures on Rhetoric and Belles Lettres*. Brooklyn, 1804.

BOK, EDWARD. *Beecher Memorial*. Brooklyn, 1887.

BORCHERS, GLADYS. *A Study of Oral Style*. Ph.D. Thesis, University of Wisconsin, 1927.

BRADFORD, GAMALIEL. *D. L. Moody: A Worker in Souls*. New York: Doubleday, Doran, 1928.

BREWSTER, W. T. *Representative Essays on Style*. New York: Macmillan Co., 1905.

BRIGANCE, W. N. *The Spoken Word*. New York: F. S. Crofts, 1927.

BROADUS, J. A. *The Preparation and Delivery of Sermons*. First ed., 1870; rev. ed., 1898.

BROOKS, PHILLIPS. *Lectures on Preaching*. New York: E. P. Dutton, 1876.

BROWN, C. R. *The Art of Preaching*. New York: Macmillan Co., 1924.

BUFFON. *Discourse sur le Style, Lane Cooper's Theories of Style*. New York: Macmillan, 1907.

CAMPBELL, GEORGE. *The Philosophy of Rhetoric*. London, 1823.

Catalogue of the bric-a-brac, rare Oriental rugs, oil paintings, furniture . . . .

and the valuable library belonging to the estate of the late Rev. Henry Ward Beecher . . . . American Art Association . . . . New York. New York: J. Little and Co., 1887.

CICERO. *De oratore.* Translated by J. S. Watson. New York: Harper & Bros., 1860.

COLERIDGE, S. T. *Literary Remains* (ed. Shedd). Vol. II. New York, 1868 .

———. *Biographia Literaria.* Shawcroft edition. Vols. I and II. Oxford University Press, 1907.

CROCKER, LIONEL. "The Rhetorical Influence of Henry Ward Beecher." *Quarterly Journal of Speech.* XVIII (February, 1932), 82–87.

———. "The Voice Element in Prose." *Quarterly Journal of Speech.* April, 1926. Pp. 168–75.

CUYLER, THEODORE L. *Recollections of a Long Life.* New York: Baker & Taylor Co., 1902.

DEMETRIUS. *On Style.* Robert's Translation. Cambridge University Press, 1902.

DE BREMONT, ANNA. "Henry Ward Beecher as an Actor." *The Theatre.* May 1, 1887.

DE QUINCEY, THOMAS. *Essays on Style, Rhetoric and Language* (ed. F. N. Scott). Boston: Allyn & Bacon, 1893.

DOWLING, JOHN. *The Power of Illustration.* New York: Colby & Co., 1850.

EARLE, JOHN. *English Prose.* London: Smith, Elder & Co., 1890.

EMERSON, R. W. *Essays.* First and second series.

FARMER, J. S., AND HENLEY, W. E. *Slang and Its Analogies.* London, 1891.

FISKE, F. W. *Manual of Preaching.* New York: Armstrong, 1893.

FORSTER, JOHN: *Life of Dickens.* Philadelphia: Lippincott, 1872.

FULLERTON, W. Y. *C. H. Spurgeon, a Biography.* London: Williams and Norgate, 1920.

FURNESS, C. J. *Walt Whitman's Workshop.* Harvard University Press, 1928.

GALSWORTHY, JOHN. *Creation of Character in Literature.* Oxford University Press, 1931.

GENUNG, J. F. *The Working Principles of Rhetoric.* New York: Ginn & Co., 1900.

GUTHRIE, THOMAS. *The Parables.* New York: E. F. Treat, 1870.

HALLIWELL, J. O. *A Dictionary of Archaic and Provincial Words*. London, 1890.

HAYNES, MARY. *The Crown of Life*. Boston: Lothrop & Co., 1890.

HENRICKSON, E. H. *Elements of Persuasion in Henry Ward Beecher's Speeches in England in 1863*. M.A. Thesis, University of Iowa, 1929.

HILLIS, NEWELL DWIGHT. *Lectures and Orations of Henry Ward Beecher*. New York: Revel, 1913.

HOLMES, OLIVER WENDELL. *Autocrat of the Breakfast Table*. New York: Houghton, Mifflin Co., 1896.

HOWARD, J., AND ELLINWOOD, T. R. *Sermon Briefs of Henry Ward Beecher*. Boston: Pilgrim Press, 1905.

HOYT, A. S. *The Work of Preaching*. New York: Macmillan & Co., 1905.

KAMES, LORD. *Elements of Criticism* (1762). New York, 1854.

KEATS, JOHN. *The Complete Works of John Keats* (ed. H. Buxton Forman). Oxford University Press, 1929.

———. *Letters*. New York: Houghton, Mifflin Co., 1899.

KNOX, T. W. *Life of Beecher*. Cincinnati, Ohio: W. E. Dibble, 1887.

LE BON, G. *The Crowd*. New York: Macmillan, 1926.

LINDSLEY, C. F. "A Footnote to Persuasion." *Quarterly Journal of Speech Education*. VII, 233–57.

LOCKE, JOHN. *Essay on Human Understanding*. New York: Dutton.

LOWES, JOHN LIVINGSTON. *The Road to Xanadu*. Boston: Houghton, Mifflin Co., 1927.

MACRAE, DAVID. *The Treasury of Modern Biography*. London: W. P. Nimmo, 1878. Pp. 445–50.

MENCKEN, H. L. *The American Language*. New York: Knopf, 1919.

MERRILL, W. P. *The Freedom of the Preacher*. New York: Macmillan Co., 1922.

MORLEY, JOHN. *Life of Gladstone*. Macmillan Co., 1903.

MORSE, J. T. *Life and Letters of Oliver Wendell Holmes*. Boston: Houghton, Mifflin Co., 1896.

MOSHER, J. A. *The Exemplum in the Early Religious and Didactic Literature in England*. Ph.D. Thesis, Columbia University Press, 1911.

———. *Complete Study of Public Speaking*. Macmillan Co., 1924.

MURRY, J. M. *The Problem of Style*. London: Oxford University Press, 1922.

New Haven Courier. February 24, 1872.

NEWMAN, JOHN. *The Idea of a University; The Works of Cardinal John Newman*. London: Longmans Green, 1923.

NEWMAN, SAMUEL P. *Practical System of Rhetoric* (1834). New York: Ivison & Phinney, 1860.

NEWTON, JOSEPH FORT. *If I Had Only One Sermon To Preach*. New York: Harper & Bros., 1932.

NORTON, SARA. *Letters of Charles Eliot Norton*. New York: Houghton, Mifflin Co., 1913.

OGDEN, C. K., AND RICHARDS, I. A. *The Meaning of Meaning*. New York: Harcourt, Brace & Co., 1927.

O'CONNOR, T. P. "Orators Who Have Influenced Me." *Harper's Weekly*. September 10, 1913.

O'NEILL, J. M., AND WEAVER, A. T. *Elements of Speech*. New York: Longmans Green, 1926.

PALMER, GEORGE HERBERT. *Self-Cultivation in English*. Boston: Houghton, Mifflin Co., 1909.

PARKHURST, C. H. *Pulpit and Pew*. Yale University Press, 1913.

PARKER, D. H. *Principles of Aesthetics*. New York: Silver, Burdette, 1920.

PARRINGTON, V. L. *The Beginnings of Realism in America*. New York: Harcourt, Brace & Co., 1930.

PARRISH, W. M. "Whately and His Rhetoric." *Quarterly Journal of Speech*. Vol. XV, No. 1, pp. 158–79.

PARTON, JAMES. *Famous Americans of Recent Times*. Boston: Ticknor & Fields, 1867.

PATTISON, T. H. *The Making of the Sermon*. Philadelphia: American Baptist Publication Society, 1898.

PERRY, BLISS. *The Heart of Emerson's Journals*. Boston: Houghton, Mifflin Co., 1909.

PHELPS, AUSTIN. *Theory of Preaching*. New York: Charles Scribner's Sons, 1885.

PHILLIPS, A. E. *Effective Speaking*. Chicago: Newton Co., 1908.

PLATO: *The Phaedrus: Five Essays on Poetic Inspiration*. Everyman Edition. New York: E. P. Dutton & Co., 1910.

POND, J. B. *A Summer in England with Henry Ward Beecher*. New York: Howard & Hulbert, 1886.

PRESCOTT, F. C. *The Poetic Mind*. London: Macmillan Co., 1926.

PUTNAM, C. *American Humor*. New York: Putnam & Sons, 1907.

QUINTILIAN. *Institutes of Oratory*. London: Bohn's Classical Library, 1873.

RALEIGH, WALTER. *Shakespeare*. London: Macmillan Co., 1924.

RANKIN, T. E., THORPE, C. D.; AND SOLVE, M. *College Composition.* New York: Harper & Bros., 1929.

RAYMOND, ROSSITER W.: *Introduction to The Crown of Life.* Boston: D. Lothrop Co., 1890.

ROBERTSON, F. W. *Sermons.* New York: Harper & Bros., 1870.

ROSS, E. A. *Social Psychology.* New York: Macmillan Co., 1908.

SANDFORD, W. P., AND YEAGER, W. H. *Principles of Effective Speaking.* New York: Thomas Nelson Sons, 1929.

SCOTT, F. N. *The Standard of American Speech and Other Papers.* New York: Allyn & Bacon, 1926.

SCOTT, W. D. *The Psychology of Public Speaking.* New York: Hinds, Noble & Eldredge, 1906.

SHURTER, E. D. *The Rhetoric of Oratory.* New York: Macmillan & Co., 1909.

SPEARMAN, C. *The Creative Mind.* New York: D. Appleton & Co., 1931.

SPENCER, HERBERT. *The Philosophy of Style* (ed. F. N. Scott). Boston: Allyn & Bacon, 1892.

SPURGEON, C. H. *The Art of Illustration.* New York: W. R. Ketcham, 1894.

STORRS, R. *Preaching without Notes.* New York: Dodd & Mead, 1875.

STOWE, HARRIET BEECHER. *Men of Our Times.* Hartford, Conn.: Hartford Publishing Co., 1868.

TAFT, H. W. *Conversation and Public Speaking.* New York: Macmillan Co., 1929.

TALMAGE, DE WITT. "Big Blunders." *Models of Speech Composition,* ed. J. M. O'Neill. New York: Century Co., 1921.

TAYLOR, W. M. *The Ministry of the Word.* New York: Randolph & Co., 1876.

TERRY, ELLEN. *The Story of My Life.* London: Hutchinson, 1913.

THORPE, C. D. "The Aesthetic Experience as Illumination." *F. N. Scott Papers.* Chicago: University of Chicago Press, 1929.

TYLER, W. S. *A History of Amherst College, 1821–1871.* Springfield, Mass., 1873.

VINET, A. *Homiletics.* New York: Ivison and Phinney, 1866.

WALLAS, GRAHAM. *The Art of Thought.* New York: Harcourt, Brace & Co., 1900.

WENDELL, BARRETT. *A Literary History of America.* New York: Scribner's Sons, 1900.

WHATELY, RICHARD. *Elements of Rhetoric* (1829). New York: Sheldon & Co., 1872.

WILLIAMSON, A. B. *Speaking in Public*. New York: Macmillan Co., 1929.

WINANS, J. A. *Public Speaking*. New York: Century Co., 1916.

WINANS, J. A., AND UTTERBACK, WILLIAM. *Argumentation*. New York: Century Co., 1930.

WILSON, THOMAS. *Art of Rhetoric*. G. H. Mair Edition. Clarendon Press, 1909.

WORDSWORTH, WILLIAM. *Preface to Lyrical Ballads* (ed. De Selincourt). Oxford University Press, 1926.

WORDSWORTH, W. *Literary Criticism*. Oxford University Press, 1925.

———. *The Prelude, or Growth of a Poet's Mind*. Boston: Heath & Co., 1888.

INDEX

INDEX

[PRINTED
  IN U·S·A]

Date Due

4038	Nov 21		
6A32	Mar 12		
6100	Dec 15		
6100	Jan 27		
6857	Dec 20		
7867	Nov 4		
NOV 11 53			
JAN 6 '54			